To My Mother

Tom Holt was born in London in 1961. At Oxford he studied bar billiards, ancient Greek agriculture and the care and feeding of small, temperamental Japanese motorcycle engines; interests which led him, perhaps inevitably, to qualify as a solicitor and emigrate to Somerset, where he specialised in death and taxes for seven years before going straight in 1995. Now a full-time writer, he lives in Chard, Somerset, with his wife, one daughter and the unmistakable scent of blood, wafting in on the breeze from the local meat-packing plant.

By Tom Holt

EXPECTING SOMEONE TALLER
WHO'S AFRAID OF BEOWULF?
FLYING DUTCH
YE GODS!
OVERTIME
HERE COMES THE SUN
GRAILBLAZERS
FAUST AMONG EQUALS
ODDS AND GODS
DJINN RUMMY
MY HERO
PAINT YOUR DRAGON
OPEN SESAME
WISH YOU WERE HERE
ONLY HUMAN
SNOW WHITE AND THE SEVEN SAMURAI

THE WALLED ORCHARD
ALEXANDER AT THE WORLD'S END

I, MARGARET

LUCIA TRIUMPHANT
LUCIA IN WARTIME

TOM HOLT

Expecting Someone Taller

ORBIT

1

After a particularly unrewarding interview with his beloved, Malcolm was driving home along a dark, winding country lane when he ran over a badger. He stopped the car and got out to inspect the damage to his paintwork and (largely from curiosity) to the badger. It was, he decided, all he needed, for there was a small but noticeable dent in his wing, and he had been hoping to sell the car.

'Damn,' he said aloud.

'So how do you think I feel?' said the badger.

Malcolm turned round quite slowly. He had had a bad day, but not so bad that he could face talking badgers – talking *dead* badgers – with equanimity. The badger was lying on its side, absolutely still. Malcolm relaxed; he must have imagined it, or perhaps the bump had accidentally switched on the car radio. Any connection was possible between the confused chow mein of wires under his dashboard.

'You're not the one who's been run over,' said the badger, bitterly.

This time, Malcolm turned round rather more quickly. There was the black and white corpse, lying across the road like a dead zebra crossing; yet he could have sworn that human speech had come from it. Was some rustic ventriloquist, possibly a Friend of the Earth, playing tricks on him? He nerved himself to examine his victim. A dead badger, nothing more, nothing less; except that there was some sort of wire contraption wrapped round its muzzle – a homing device, perhaps, attached by a questing ecologist.

'Did you say something?' said Malcolm, nervously.

'So you're not deaf as well as blind,' said the badger. 'Yes, I did say something. Why don't you pay more attention when people talk to you?'

Malcolm felt rather embarrassed. His social equipment did not include formulae for talking to people he had just mortally wounded, or badgers, let alone a combination of the two. Nevertheless, he felt it incumbent upon him to say something, and his mind hit upon the word designed for unfamiliar situations.

'Sorry,' he said.

'You're sorry,' said the badger. 'The hell with you.'

There was a silence, broken only by the screech of a distant owl. After a while, Malcolm came to the conclusion that the badger *was* dead, and that during the collision he had somehow concussed himself without noticing it. Either that, or it was a dream. He had heard about people who fell asleep at the wheel, and remembered that they usually crashed and killed themselves. That did not cheer him up particularly.

'Anyway,' said the badger, 'what's your name?'

'Malcolm,' said Malcolm. 'Malcolm Fisher.'

'Say that again,' said the badger. 'Slowly.'

'Mal-colm Fi-sher.'

The badger was silent for a moment. 'Are your sure?' it said, sounding rather puzzled.

'Yes,' said Malcolm. 'Sorry.'

'Well, Malcolm Fisher, let's have a look at you.'

The badger twisted its head painfully round, and looked at him in silence for a while. 'You know,' it said at last, 'I was expecting someone rather taller.'

'Oh,' said Malcolm.

'Fair-haired, tall, muscular, athletic, without spectacles,' went on the badger. 'Younger, but also more mature, if you see what I mean. Someone with presence. Someone you'd notice if you walked into a room full of strangers. In fact, you're a bit of a disappointment.'

2

There was no answer to that, except Sorry again, and that would be a stupid thing to say. Nevertheless, it was irritating to have one's physical shortcomings pointed out quite so plainly twice in one evening, once by a beautiful girl and once by a dying badger. 'So what?' said Malcolm, uppishly.

'All right,' said the badger. 'Sorry I spoke, I'm sure. Well, now you're here, you might as well get it over with. Though I'm not sure it's not cheating hitting me with that thing.' And it waved a feeble paw at Malcolm's aged Renault.

'Get what over with?' asked Malcolm.

'Don't let's play games,' said the badger. 'You've killed me, you needn't mess me around as well. Take the Ring and the Tarnhelm and piss off.'

'I don't follow,' said Malcolm. 'What are you talking about?'

The badger jerked violently, and spasms of pain ran through its shattered body. 'You mean it was an *accident*?' it rasped. 'After nearly a thousand years, it's a bloody accident. Marvellous!' The dying animal made a faint gasping noise that might just have been the ghost of laughter.

'Now you have lost me,' said Malcolm.

'I'd better hurry up, then,' said the badger, with weary resignation in its voice. 'Unless you want me dying on you, that is, before I can tell you the story. Take that wire gadget off my nose.'

Gingerly, Malcolm stretched out his fingers, fully expecting the beast to snap at them. Badgers' jaws, he remembered, are immensely strong. But the animal lay still and patient, and he was able to pull the wire net free. At once the badger disappeared, and in its place there lay a huge, grey-haired man, at least seven feet tall, with cruel blue eyes and a long, tangled beard.

'That's better,' he said. 'I hated being a badger. Fleas.'

'I'd better get you to a hospital,' said Malcolm.

'Don't bother,' said the giant. 'Human medicine

3

wouldn't work on me anyway. My heart is in my right foot, my spine is made of chalcedony, and my intestines are soluble in aspirin. I'm a Giant, you see. In fact I am – was – the last of the Giants.'

The Giant paused, like a television personality stepping out into the street and waiting for the first stare of recognition.

'How do you mean, Giant, exactly? You're very tall, but . . .'

The Giant closed his eyes and moaned softly.

'Come on,' said Malcolm, 'there's a casualty department in Taunton. We can get there in forty minutes.'

The Giant ignored him. 'Since you are totally ignorant of even basic theogony,' he said, 'I will explain. My name is Ingolf, and I am the last of the Frost-Giants of the Elder Age.'

'Pleased to meet you,' said Malcolm instinctively.

'Are you hell as like. I am the youngest brother of Fasolt and Fafner the castle-builders. Does that ring a bell? No?'

'No.'

'You didn't even see the opera?' said Ingolf, despairingly.

'I'm afraid I'm not a great fan of opera,' said Malcolm, 'so it's unlikely.'

'I don't believe it. Well, let's not go into all that now. I'll be dead in about three minutes. When you get home, look up the Ring Cycle in your *Boy's Book of Knowledge*. My story starts with the last act of *Götterdämmerung*. The funeral pyre. Siegfried lying in state. On his belt, the Tarnhelm. On his finger, the Nibelung's Ring.' Ingolf paused. 'Sorry, am I boring you?'

'No,' Malcolm said. 'Go on, please.'

'Hagen snatches the Ring from Siegfried's hand as Brunnhilde plunges into the heart of the fire. At once, the Rhine bursts its banks – I'd been warning them about that embankment for years, but would they listen? – and the Rhinedaughters drag Hagen down into the depths of the

4

river and drown him. For no readily apparent reason, Valhalla catches fire. Tableau. The End. Except,' and Ingolf chuckled hoarsely through his tattered lungs, 'the stupid tarts dropped the ring while they were drowning Hagen, and guess who was only a few feet away, clinging to a fallen tree, as I recall. Me. Ingolf. Ingolf the Neglected, Ingolf the Patient, Ingolf, Heir to the Ring! So I grabbed it, pulled the Tarnhelm from the ashes of the pyre, and escaped in the confusion. To here, in fact, the Vale of Taunton Deane. Last place God made, but never mind.'

'Fascinating,' said Malcolm after a while. 'That doesn't explain why you were a badger just now, and why you aren't one any longer.'

'Doesn't it?' Ingolf groaned again. 'The Tarnhelm, you ignorant child, is a magic cap made by Mime, the greatest craftsman in history. Whoever wears it can take any shape or form he chooses, animate or inanimate, man, bird or beast, rock, tree or flower. Or he can be invisible, or transport himself instantaneously from one end of the earth to the other, just by thinking. And this idiot here thought, Who would come looking for a badger? So I turned myself into one and came to this godforsaken spot to hide.'

'Why?'

'Because it's godforsaken, and I'd had about as much of the Gods as I could take. They were after me, you see. In fact, they probably still are. Also the Volsungs. And the Rhinemaidens. And Alberich. The whole bloody lot of them. It hasn't been easy, I can tell you. Luckily, they're all so unbelievably *stupid*. They've spent the last thousand odd years searching high and low for a ninety-foot dragon with teeth like standing stones and an enormous tail. Just because my brother Fafner – a pleasant enough chap in his way, but scarcely imaginative – disguised *him*self as a dragon when he had the perishing thing. I could have told him that a ninety-foot dragon was scarcely inconspicuous, even in the Dawn of the World, but why should I help him?

5

Anyway, I very sensibly became a badger and outsmarted them all.'

'Hang on,' said Malcolm, 'I'm a bit confused. Why did you have to hide?'

'Because,' said Ingolf, 'they wanted the Ring.'

'So why didn't you give it to them – whoever they were – and save yourself all the bother?'

'Whoever owns the ring is the master of the world,' said Ingolf, gravely.

'Oh,' said Malcolm. 'So you're . . .'

'And a fat lot of good it's done me, you might very well say. Who did you think ruled the world, anyway, the United bloody Nations?'

'I hadn't given it much thought, to be honest with you. But if you're the ruler of the world . . .'

'I know what you're thinking. If I'm master of the world, why should I have to hide in a copse in Somerset disguised as a badger?'

'More or less,' said Malcolm.

'Uneasy lies the head that wears a crown,' said the Giant sagely. 'Looking back, of course, I sometimes wonder whether it was all worth it. But you will learn by my mistakes.'

Malcolm furrowed his brow. 'You mean you're leaving them all to me?' he asked. 'The Ring and the – what did you say it was called?'

'Tarnhelm. It means helmet of darkness, though why they describe it as a helmet when it's just a little scrap of wire I couldn't tell you. Anyway, take them with my blessing, for what that's worth.'

Ingolf paused to catch his breath.

'To gain inexhaustible wealth,' he continued, 'just breathe on the Ring and rub it gently on your forehead. Go on, try it.'

Ingolf eased the plain gold ring off his finger and passed it to Malcolm, who accepted it rather as one might accept some delicacy made from the unspeakable parts of a rare amphibian at an embassy function. He did as Ingolf told him, and at once found himself knee-deep in gold. Gold cups, gold plates, gold brooches, pins, bracelets, anklets, pectorals, cruets and sauce-boats.

'Convinced?' said Ingolf. 'Or do you want a metallurgist's report?'

'I believe you,' said Malcolm, who was indeed firmly convinced that he was dreaming, and vowed never to eat Stilton cheese late at night again.

'Leave them,' said Ingolf. 'Plenty more where that came from. The Nibelungs make them in the bottomless caverns of Nibelheim, the Kingdom of the Mists. They'll be glad of the warehouse space.'

'And the Tarnhelm – that works too, does it?'

Ingolf finally seemed to lose patience. 'Of course it bloody works,' he shouted. 'Put it on and turn yourself into a human being.'

'Sorry,' said Malcolm. 'It's all been rather a shock.'

'Finally,' said Ingolf, 'cut my arm and lick some of the blood.'

'I'd rather not,' said Malcolm, firmly.

'If you do, you'll be able to understand the language of the birds.'

'I don't particularly want to be able to understand the language of the birds,' said Malcolm.

'You'll understand the language of the birds and like it, my lad,' said Ingolf severely. 'Now do as you are told. Use the pin on one of those brooches there.'

The blood tasted foul and was burning hot. For a second, Malcolm's brain clouded over; then, faintly in the distance, he heard the owl hoot again, and realised to his astonishment that he could understand what it was saying. Not that it was saying anything of any interest, of course.

'Oh,' said Malcolm. 'Oh, well, thank you.'

'Now then,' said the Giant. 'I am about to go on my last journey. Pile up that gold around my head. I must take it with me to pay the ferryman.'

'I thought it was just a coin on the eyes or something.'

'Inflation. Also, I'll take up rather a lot of room on the boat.' He scowled. 'Get on with it, will you?' he said. 'Or do you want a receipt?'

Malcolm did as he was told. After all, it wasn't as if it was real gold. Was it?

'Listen,' said Ingolf, 'listen carefully. I am dying now. When I am dead, my body will turn back into the living rock from which Lord Ymir moulded the race of the Frost-Giants when the world was young. Nothing will grow here for a thousand years, and horses will throw their riders when they pass the spot. Pity, really, it's a main road. Oh, well. Every year, on the anniversary of my death, fresh blood will well up out of the earth and the night air will be filled with uncanny cries. That is the Weird of the Ring-Bearer when his life is done. Be very careful, Malcolm Fisher. There is a curse on the Nibelung's Ring – the curse of Alberich, which brings all who wear it to a tragic and untimely death. Yet it is fated that when the Middle Age of the world is drawing to a close, a foolish, godlike boy who does not understand the nature of the Ring will break the power of Alberich's curse and thereby redeem the world. Then the Last Age of the world will begin, the Gods will go down for ever, and all things shall be well.' Ingolf's eyes were closing, his breath was faint, his words scarcely audible. But suddenly he started, and propped himself up on one elbow.

'Hold on a minute,' he gasped. 'A foolish, godlike boy who does not understand . . . who does not understand . . .' He sank down again, his strength exhausted. 'Still,' he said, 'I was expecting someone rather taller.'

He shuddered for the last time, and was as still as stone. The wind, which had been gathering during his last speech, started to scream, lashing the trees into a frenzy. The Giant was dead; already his shape was unrecognisable as his body turned back into grey stone, right in the middle of the Minehead to Bridgwater trunk road. All around him,

8

Malcolm could hear a confused babble of voices, human and animal, living and dead, and, like the counterpoint to a vast fugue, the low, rumbling voices of the trees and the rocks. The entire earth was repeating the astonishing news: Ingolf was dead, the world had a new master.

Just then, two enormous ravens flapped slowly and lazily over Malcolm's head. He stood paralysed with inexplicable fear, but the ravens flew on. The voices died away, the wind dropped, the rain subsided. As soon as he was able to move, Malcolm jumped in his car and drove home as fast as the antiquated and ill-maintained engine would permit him to go. He undressed in the dark and fell into bed, and was soon fast asleep and dreaming a strange and terrible dream, all about being trapped in a crowded lift with no trousers on. Suddenly he woke up and sat bolt upright in the darkness. On his finger was the Ring. Beside his bed, between his watch and his key-chain, was the Tarnhelm. Outside his window, a nightingale was telling another nightingale what it had had for lunch.

'Oh my God,' said Malcolm, and went back to sleep.

The Oberkasseler Bridge over the Rhine has acquired a sinister reputation in recent years, and the two policemen who were patrolling it knew this only too well. They knew what to look for, and they seldom had to look far in this particular area.

A tall man with long grey hair falling untidily over the collar of his dark blue suit leaned against the parapet eating an ice cream. Although impeccably dressed, he was palpably all wrong, and the two policemen looked at each other with pleasant anticipation.

'Drugs?' suggested the first policeman.

'More like dirty books,' said the other. 'If he's armed, it's my turn.'

'It's always your turn,' grumbled his companion.

The first policeman shrugged his shoulders. 'Oh, all right then,' he said. 'But I get to drive back to the station.'

But as they approached their prey, they began to feel distinctly uncomfortable. It was not fear but a sort of awe or respect that caused them to hesitate as the tall man turned and stared at them calmly through his one eye. Suddenly, they found that they were having difficulty breathing.

'Excuse me, sir,' said the first policeman, gasping slightly, 'can you tell me the time?'

'Certainly,' said the tall man, without looking at his watch, 'it's just after half-past eleven.'

The two policemen turned and walked away quickly. As they did so, they both simultaneously looked at their own watches. Twenty-eight minutes to twelve.

'He must have been looking at the clock,' said the first policeman.

'What clock?' inquired his companion, puzzled.

'I don't know. Any bloody clock.'

The tall man turned and gazed down at the brown river for a while. Then he clicked his fingers, and a pair of enormous ravens floated down and landed on either side of him on the parapet. The tall man broke little pieces off the rim of his cornet and flicked them at the two birds as he questioned them.

'Any luck?' he asked.

'What do you think?' replied the smaller of the two.

'Keep trying,' said the tall man calmly. 'Have you done America today?'

The smaller raven's beak was full of cornet, so the larger raven, although unused to being the spokesman, said Yes, they had. No luck.

'We checked America,' said the smaller raven, 'and Africa, and Asia, and Australasia, and Europe. Bugger all, same as always.'

'Maybe you were looking in the wrong place,' suggested the tall man.

'You don't understand,' said the smaller raven. 'It's like looking for . . .' the bird racked its brains for a suitably graphic simile '. . . for a needle in a haystack,' it concluded triumphantly.

'Well,' said the tall man, 'I suggest you go and look again. Carefully, this time. My patience is beginning to wear a little thin.'

Suddenly he closed his broad fist around the cornet, crushing it into flakes and dust.

'You've got ice cream all over your hand,' observed the larger raven.

'So I have,' said the tall man. 'Now get out, and this time concentrate.'

The ravens flapped their broad, drab wings and floated away. Frowning, the tall man clicked the fingers of his clean hand and took out his handkerchief.

'I've got a tissue if you'd rather use it,' said a nervous-looking thin man who had hurried up to him. The tall man waved it away.

'How about you?' he asked the thin man. 'Done any good?'

'Nothing. I did Toronto, Lusaka, and Brasilia. Have you ever been to Brasilia? Last place God made. Oh, I'm sorry. I didn't mean . . .'

'The more I think about it,' said the tall man, ignoring this gaffe, 'the more convinced I am that he's still in Europe. When Ingolf went to ground, the other continents hadn't even been discovered.'

The thin man looked puzzled. 'Ingolf?' he said. 'Haven't you heard?'

The tall man turned his head and fixed him with his one eye. The thin man started to tremble slightly, for he knew that expression well.

'Ingolf is dead,' continued the thin man. 'I thought you'd have known.'

The tall man was silent. Clouds, which had not been there a moment before, passed in front of the sun.

'I'm only the King of the Gods, nobody ever bothers to tell me anything,' said the tall man. 'So?'

'He died at a quarter to midnight last night, at a place called Ralegh's Cross in the West of England. He was knocked down by a car, and . . .'

11

Rain was falling now, hard and straight, but the thin man was sweating. Oddly enough, the tall man wasn't getting wet.

'No sign of the Ring,' said the thin man nervously. 'Or the helmet. I've checked all the usual suspects, but they don't seem to have heard or seen anything. In fact, they were as surprised as you were. I mean . . .'

Thunder now, and a flicker of distant lightning.

'I got there as quickly as I could,' said the thin man, desperately. 'As soon as I felt the shock. But I was in Brasilia, like I said, and it takes time . . .'

'All the usual suspects?'

'All of them. Every one.'

Suddenly, the tall man smiled. The rain stopped, and a rainbow flashed across the sky.

'I believe you,' said the tall man, 'thousands wouldn't. Right, so if it wasn't one of the usual suspects, it must have been an outsider, someone we haven't dealt with before. That should make it all much easier. So start searching.'

'Anywhere in particular?'

'Use your bloody imagination,' growled the tall man, irritably, and the rainbow promptly faded away. The thin man smiled feebly, and soon was lost to sight among the passers-by. Wotan, the great Sky-God and King of all the Gods, put his handkerchief back in his pocket and gazed up into the sky, where the two enormous ravens were circling.

'Got all that?' Wotan murmured.

Thought, the elder and smaller of the two messenger ravens who are the God's eyes and ears on earth, dipped his wings to show that he had, and Wotan walked slowly away.

'Like looking for a needle in a haystack,' repeated Thought, sliding into a convenient thermal. His younger brother, Memory, banked steeply and followed him.

'This is true,' replied Memory, 'definitely.'

'You know the real trouble with this business?' said Memory, diving steeply after a large moth.

'What's that, then?'

'Bloody awful industrial relations, that's what. I mean, take Wotan. Thinks he's God almighty.'

'He is, isn't he?'

Memory hovered for a moment on a gust of air. 'I never thought of that,' he said at last.

'Well, you wouldn't,' said Thought, 'would you?'

2

The next morning, Malcolm thought long and hard before waking up, for he had come to recognise over the past quarter of a century that rather less can go wrong if you are asleep.

But the radiant light of a brilliant summer morning, shining in through the window in front of which he had neglected to draw the curtains, chased away all possibility of sleep, and Malcolm was left very much awake, although still rather confused. Such confusion was, however, his normal state of mind. Without it, he would feel rather lost.

Confusion is the only possible result of a lifetime of being asked unanswerable questions by one's parents and relatives, such as 'What *are* we going to do with you?' or 'Why can't you be more like your sister?' To judge by the frequency with which he encountered it, the latter problem was the truly significant one, to which not even the tremendous intellectual resources of his family had been able to find an answer. Malcolm himself had never made any sort of attempt to solve this problem; that was not his role in life. His role (if he had one, which he sometimes doubted) was to provide a comparison with his elder sister Bridget. Rather like the control group in the testing process for a new medicine, Malcolm was there to ensure that his parents never took their exceptional daughter for granted. If ever they were misguided enough to doubt or under-estimate that glorious creature, one look at Malcolm was enough to remind them how lucky they were, so it was Malcolm's calling to be a disappointment; he would be failing in his duty as a son and a brother if he was anything else.

When Bridget had married Timothy (a man who perfectly exemplified the old saying that all work and no play makes Jack a management consultant) and gone to turn the rays of her effulgence on Sydney, Australia, it was therefore natural that her parents, lured by the prospect of grandchildren to persecute, should sell all they had and follow her. They had muttered something about Malcolm presumably coming too, but their heart was not really in it; he was no longer needed, now that the lacklustre Timothy could take over the mantle of unworthiness. So Malcolm had decided that he would prefer to stay in England. He disliked bright sunlight, had no great interest in the cinema, opera, tennis or seafood, and didn't particularly want to go on getting under people's feet for the rest of his life. He was thus able to add ingratitude and lack of proper filial and brotherly affection to the already impressive list of things that were wrong with him but not with his sister.

After a great deal of enjoyable agonising, Mr and Mrs Fisher decided that Malcolm's only chance of ever amounting to anything was being made to stand on his own two feet, and allowed him to stay behind. Before they left, however, they went to an extraordinary amount of trouble and effort to find him a boring job and a perfectly horrible flat in a nasty village in the middle of nowhere. So it was that Malcolm had come to leave his native Derby, a place he had never greatly cared for, and go into the West, almost (but not quite) like King Arthur. Taking with him his good suit, his respectable shirts, his spongebag and his two A-levels, he had made his way to Somerset, where he had been greeted with a degree of enthusiasm usually reserved for the first drop of rain at a Wimbledon final by his parents' long-suffering contacts, whose tireless efforts had made his new life possible. Malcolm took to the trade of an auctioneer's clerk like a duck to petrol, found the local dialect

15

almost as inscrutable as the locals found his own slight accent, and settled down, like Kent in *King Lear*, to shape his old course in a country new.

The fact that he hated and feared his new environment was largely beside the point, for he had been taught long ago that what he thought and felt about any given subject was without question the least important thing in the world. Indeed he had taken this lesson so much to heart that when the Government sent him little pieces of card apparently entitling him to vote in elections, he felt sure that they had intended them for somebody else. He told himself that he would soon get used to it, just as he had always been told that he would grow into the grotesquely outsized garments he was issued with as a child. Although two years had now passed since his arrival in the West Country, the sleeves of his new life, so to speak, still reached down to his fingernails. But that was presumably his fault for not growing. Needless to say, it was a remark of his sister Bridget's that best summed up his situation; to be precise, a joke she used to make at the age of seven. 'What is the difference,' she would ask, 'between Marmalade [the family cat] and Malcolm?' When no satisfactory answer could be provided by the admiring adults assembled to hear the joke, Bridget would smile and say, 'Daddy isn't allowed to shout at Marmalade.'

So it seemed rather strange (or counter-intuitive, as his sister would say) that Malcolm should have been chosen by the badger to be the new master of the world. Bridget, yes; she was very good indeed at organising things, and would doubtless make sure that the trains ran on time. But Malcolm – 'only Malcolm', as he was affectionately known to his family – that was a mistake, surely. Still, he reflected as he put the Ring back on his finger, since he was surely imagining the whole thing, what did it matter?

Without bothering to get out of bed, he breathed on the Ring and rubbed it on his forehead. At once, countless gold objects materialised in the air and fell heavily all around

16

him, taking him so completely by surprise that all he could think was that this must be what the Americans mean by a shower. Gold cups, gold plates, gold chalices, torques, ashtrays, pipe-racks, cufflinks, bath-taps, and a few shapeless, unformed articles (presumably made by apprentice Nibelungs at evening classes under the general heading of paperweights) tumbled down on all sides, so that Malcolm had to snatch up a broad embossed dish and hold it over his head until the cascade had subsided in order to avoid serious injury.

Gathering the shreds of his incredulity around him, Malcolm tried to tell himself that it probably wasn't real or solid gold; but that was a hard hypothesis. Only a complete and utter cheapskate would go to the trouble of materialising copper or brass by supernatural means. No, it was real, it was solid, it existed, and it was making the place look like a scrapyard, as his mother would undoubtedly say were she present. Having wriggled out from under the hoard, Malcolm found some cardboard boxes and put it all neatly away. That alone was hard work. Malcolm shook his head, yawned, and wiped the sweat from his forehead with the back of his hand, thus accidentally starting off the whole process all over again . . .

'For Christ's sake!' he shouted, as a solid gold ewer missed him by inches, 'will you stop that?'

The torrent ceased, and Malcolm sat down on the bed.

'Well, I'm damned,' he said aloud, as he removed a gold tie-pin that had fallen into his pyjama pocket. 'Ruler of the world . . .'

Try as he might, he couldn't get the concept to make sense, so he put it aside. There was also the Tarnhelm to consider. Very, very tentatively, he put it on and stood in front of the mirror. It covered his head – it seemed to have grown in the night, or did it expand and contract automatically to fit its owner? – and was fastened under the chin by a little buckle in the shape of a crouching gnome.

So far as he could remember, all he had to do was think of

17

something he wanted to be, or a place he wanted to go to, and the magic cap did all the rest. As usual when asked to think of something, Malcolm's mind went completely blank. He stood for a while, perplexed, then recalled that the helmet could also make him invisible. He thought invisible. He was.

It was a strange sensation to look in the mirror and not see oneself, and Malcolm was not sure that he liked it. So he decided to reappear and was profoundly relieved when he saw his reflection in the glass once more. He repeated the process a couple of times, appearing and disappearing like a trafficator, now you see me, now you don't, and so on. Childish, he said to himself. We must take this thing seriously or else go stark staring mad.

Next, he must try shape-changing proper. He looked round the room for inspiration, and his eye fell on an old newspaper with a photograph of the Chancellor of the Exchequer on the front page. The thought crossed his mind that his mother had always wanted him to make something of himself, and now if he wanted to, he could be a member of the Cabinet . . .

In the mirror, he caught sight of the Chancellor of the Exchequer, looking perhaps a trifle eccentric in blue pyjamas and a chain-mail cap, but nevertheless unmistakable. Even though he had done his best to prepare his mind for the experience of shape-changing, the shock was terrifying in its intensity. He looked frantically round the room to see if he could see himself anywhere, but no sign. He had actually changed shape.

He forced himself to look at the reflection in the mirror, and it occurred to him that if he was going to do this sort of thing at all, he might as well do it properly. He concentrated his mind and thought of the Chancellor in his customary dark grey suit. At once, the reflection changed, and now the only jarring note was the chain-mail cap. That might well be a problem if it insisted on remaining visible all the time. He could wear a hat over it, he supposed, but that would be tricky indoors, and so few people wore hats these days. Malcolm thought how nice it would be if the cap could make itself invisible. At once, it disappeared, giving an excellent view of the Chancellor's thinning grey hair. So the thing worked. Nevertheless, he reflected, it would be necessary to think with unaccustomed precision when using it.

Once he had overcome his initial fear of the Tarnhelm, Malcolm set about testing it thoroughly. Had anyone been sufficiently inquisitive, or sufficiently interested in Malcolm Fisher, to be spying on him with a pair of binoculars, they would have seen him change himself into the entire Cabinet, the King of Swaziland, Theseus, and Winston Churchill, all in under a minute. But it then occurred to him that he need not restrict himself to specific people. The only piece of equipment with similar potential he had ever encountered was a word-processor, and there was not even a manual he could consult. How would it be if the Tarnhelm could do Types?

'Make me,' he said aloud, 'as handsome as it is possible to be.'

He closed his eyes, not daring to look, then opened his right eye slowly. Then his left eye, rather more quickly. The result was pleasing, to say the least. For some reason best known to itself, the Tarnhelm had chosen to clothe this paradigm in some barbaric costume from an earlier era – probably to show the magnificent chest and shoulders off to their best advantage. But England is a cold place, even in what is supposed to be summer . . . 'Try that in a cream suit,' he suggested, 'and rather shorter hair. And lose the beard.'

He stood for a while and stared. The strange thing was that he felt completely comfortable with this remarkable new shape; in fact, he could not remember exactly what he actually looked like, himself, in propria persona. The first time he had ever been aware of his own appearance (so far as he could recall) was when he appeared in a school

19

nativity play, typecast as Eighth Shepherd, at the age of five. He had had to stand in front of a mirror to do up his cloak, and had suddenly realised that the rather ordinary child in the glass was himself. Quite naturally, he had burst out crying, refusing to be comforted, so that the Second King had had to go on for him and say his one line (which was, he seemed to recall, 'Oh look!').

'I'll take it,' he said to the mirror, and nodded his head to make the reflection agree with him. He then hurried through every permutation of clothes and accessories, just to make sure. There was no doubt about it; the Tarnhelm had very good taste. 'We'll call that one Richard' (he had always wanted to be called Richard). He resumed his own shape (which came as a bitter disappointment) then said 'Richard', firmly. At once, the Most Handsome Man reappeared in the mirror, which proved that the Tarnhelm had a memory, like a pocket calculator.

'How about,' he said diffidently, 'the most beautiful *woman* in the world? Just for fun,' he added quickly.

Contrary to all his expectations, the Tarnhelm did as it was told, and the mirror was filled with a vision of exquisite loveliness, so that it took Malcolm some time to realise that it was him. In fact the extraordinary thing was that all this seemed perfectly natural. Why shouldn't he be what he wanted to be, and to hell with the laws of physics?

The next stage was to test the cap's travel mode. Ingolf had told him that he could enjoy instantaneous and unlimited travel, and although this sounded rather like a prize in a game show or an advertisement for a season ticket, he was fully prepared to believe that it was possible. If he was going out, however, he ought to get dressed, for he was still in his pyjamas. He looked around for some clean socks, then remembered that it wasn't necessary. He could simply think himself dressed, and no need to worry about clean shirts. In fact, he could now have that rather nice cashmere sweater he had seen in that shop in Bridgwater, and no problem about getting one in his size, either.

For his first journey it would be advisable not to be too ambitious, just in case there were complications. 'The bathroom,' he thought, and there he was. No sensation of rushing through the air or dissolving particle by particle; he was just there. Rather a disappointment, for Malcolm enjoyed travel, and it is better to travel hopefully than to arrive (or at least that had always been his experience). 'The High Street,' he commanded.

It was cold out in the street, and he had to call for an overcoat, which came at once, slipping imperceptibly over his shoulders and doing up its buttons of its own accord. 'Back,' he thought, and he was sitting on his bed once again. Suddenly, this too seemed intensely real, and it was the ease with which he managed it that made it seem so; no difficulty, as one might expect from a conjuring-trick or a sleight of hand. He transformed himself and travelled through space as easily as he moved the fingers of his hand, and by exactly the same process; he willed it to happen and it happened. In the same way, it seemed to lose its enchantment. Just because one is able to move one's arms simply by wanting to, it does not follow that one continually does so just for the fun of it. He felt somehow disillusioned, and had to make a conscious effort to continue with the experiment.

It occurred to him that he had not actually specified where he wanted to be put down in the High Street. This could lead to problems. If he were to say 'Jamaica' or 'Finland' without specifying where exactly in those particular countries he wished to end up, he might find himself standing on the surface of a lake or the fast lane of a motorway. He tried the High Street again, and found that he was exactly half-way up it, and standing safely on the pavement. He repeated the procedure three times, and each time ended up in the same spot. Then he tried a few of the neighbouring towns and villages. A distinct pattern emerged. The Tarnhelm put him as close as it reasonably could to the centre of the town, and in every instance in a

21

place of safety where he could materialise without being noticed.

Could he combine shape-changing and travel? 'Bristol and a postman,' he cried, and a postman in the centre of Bristol he became. This was enjoyable. He rattled through the capital cities of the world (as many as he could remember; he had done badly at geography at school) in a variety of disguises, pausing only for a moment in each place to find a shop-window in which to see his reflection. The only failure – relative failure – in this procession was Washington, which he had elected to visit in the guise of a computer programmer. He forgot to specify which Washington, and the Tarnhelm, doubtless on the principle of *difficilior lectio*, had sent him to Tyne and Wear.

He had almost forgotten in all this excitement that he was also supposed to be able to understand the language of the birds. When he had returned to Nether Stowey, he overheard snatches of conversation outside the window, which worried him until he realised that it was in fact a pair of seriously-minded crows who were discussing the world situation, with special reference to the death of Ingolf. This reminded Malcolm that he really ought to find out a little more about the background to his new possessions. So he went, invisibly and instantaneously, to the library and spent an hour or so reading through the libretti of Wagner's operas.

Rather than wade through the text, which was German poetry translated into some obscure dialect of Middle English, he read through the synopses of the plot, and highly improbable he found it all. The fact that it was all (apparently) true did little to improve matters. Malcolm had never been greatly inclined to metaphysical or religious speculation, but he had hoped that if there was a supreme being or divine agency, it would at least show the elements of logic and common sense in its conduct. Seemingly, not so. On the other hand, the revelation that the destiny of the world had been shaped by a bunch of verbose idiots went some way towards explaining the problems of human existence.

For one could attribute any sort of illogical folly to a god who orders a castle to be built for him by a couple of Frost-Giants in the full knowledge that the price he is expected to pay for his new home is his sister-in-law. But this, apparently, was what Wotan, the great Sky-God and King of the Gods, had seen fit to do, promising his wife's sister Freia to the Giants Fasolt and Fafner. Arguably an arrangement by which one gains a castle and disposes of a relative by marriage at one and the same time is a bargain in anybody's terms; but Wotan, if this was at the back of his omniscient mind, had apparently overlooked the fact that this Freia was the guardian of the golden apples of youth, through whose power the Gods not only kept the doctor away but also maintained their immortality. Without Freia to supply them with golden apples, they would all dry up and perish, and the Giants, who appeared to have at least an elementary grounding in politics, philosophy and economics, were well aware of this when they struck the bargain.

Something of a dilemma for the everlasting Gods. But to their aid comes the clever Fire-God, Loge, who persuades the Giants that what they really need is not the most beautiful woman in the world, who also happens to be the guardian of the secret of eternal youth, but a small, plain gold ring that belongs to somebody else. The Ring is, in fact, the property of Alberich, a sulphur-dwarf from the underground caverns of Nibelheim.

Alberich had stolen some magic gold from the River Rhine, wherein dwelt (presumably before the river became polluted) three rather pretty girls, the Rhinedaughters, who owned the magic gold. This gold, if made into a ring by someone who vowed to do without Love (some of us, Malcolm reflected bitterly, have no choice in the matter),

23

would confer upon its owner the control of the world, in some concrete but ill-defined way. Alberich had originally set out with the intention of chatting up one of the Rhinedaughters; having failed in this, he cursed Love, stole the gold, and made the Ring. By its power, he found that he was able to compel all his fellow sulphur-dwarves to mine and work gold for him in unlimited quantities, this apparently being what sulphur-dwarves do best. With this wealth, it was his intention to subvert the world and make himself its master.

Before he can get very far with this project, Wotan steals the Ring from him and uses it to pay off the Giants, who immediately start fighting over who should have it. Fafner kills Fasolt, and transforms himself into a dragon before retiring to a cave in a forest in the middle of nowhere, this apparently being preferable in his eyes to retiring to a cave in a forest with the Goddess Freia. It takes all sorts.

Wotan is understandably concerned to get hold of the Ring for himself. Once again, Malcolm was moved to wonder at the stupidity, or at least the obscurity, of the King of the Gods; evidently the sort of person who, if asked to rescue a cat from a roof, would tackle the problem by burning the house down. Wotan sets about securing the ring by having an affair with Mother Earth, the result of which is nine noisy daughters called Valkyries, and a son and a daughter called Volsungs. The latter obviously take after their father, for all they manage to do before meeting with horrible deaths is commit incest and produce a son.

This son is Siegfried, a muscular but stupid youth who kills the dragon Fafner. From the pile of gold on top of which the dragon has been sleeping for a hundred years (rather uncomfortable, Malcolm thought), Siegfried picks out the Ring and the Tarnhelm, not knowing what they are for. He only discovers the secret of these articles when, led by a woodbird, he wakes up the Number One Valkyrie, Brunnhilde, who has been sleeping on a fiery mountain for twenty years after a quarrel with her father.

Brunnhilde, who is of course Siegfried's *aunt*, is also the first woman he has ever seen, and the two of them fall in love at first sight. Brunnhilde tells Siegfried all about the Ring and the terrible curse that Alberich had placed on it which brings all who own it to a horrible and untimely death. Siegfried, not being a complete idiot, gives it to her as a present. This is, of course, all in accordance with Wotan's plan ('Sounds more like coincidence to me,' said Malcolm to himself, 'but never mind') since Brunnhilde is the embodiment of Wotan's will, and because Wotan is forbidden by his intermittent but ferocious conscience to touch the perishing thing himself, Brunnhilde getting it is the nearest he can come to controlling it.

In a logical world, that would be that. But Siegfried goes off into the world to continue his career as a professional Hero, and falls in with some very dubious people called the Gibichungs. They manage to persuade Siegfried to take the Ring back from Brunnhilde and marry their horse-faced sister Gutrune. Brunnhilde is naturally livid, and conspires with Hagen (a Gibichung and also, would you believe, Alberich's son) to kill Siegfried and get the Ring back. Hagen kills Siegfried, and Brunnhilde immediately changes her mind (so like a woman). She hurls herself onto Siegfried's funeral pyre, clutching the Ring, and is burnt to a crisp. As she does so, the Rhine fortuitously bursts its banks and floods Germany, allowing the Rhinedaughters to snatch the Ring from Brunnhilde's charred finger and drown Hagen. Meanwhile, the castle of the Gods (which had caused the whole mess in the first place) has caught fire and burns down, the Gods rather foolishly neglecting to leave it while it does so, and the curtain falls on a car-bonised heaven and a flooded earth, or, in other words, a typical operatic Happy Ending. Or so Wagner thought . . .

Having finally come to the end of this narrative, Malcolm was left with two abiding impressions: first, that Fafner the dragon, instead of keeping his money under the mattress like everyone else, had kept his mattress under the money; second, that humanity generally gets the Gods it deserves. He shook his head sadly and transported himself to the pub.

Over a pint of beer and a chicken sandwich, he went over the story in his mind. The logical flaws and inconsistencies that riddled the tale, far from making him doubt its veracity, finally convinced him that it might indeed be true; for life is like that. He also wrote down on a beer-mat the names of all the Gods and monsters who might come looking for him, and turned his attention to more pressing matters.

First, there was the problem of turning the Nibelung's gold into folding money. He resolved to try the straightforward approach, and so transported himself to Bond Street, where he found an old-established jeweller's shop. He assumed a grave and respectable appearance and approached the counter holding two heavy gold chalices selected at random from the gold he had materialised that morning. The jeweller studied them for a moment in silence.

'That's odd,' he said, turning one of them over in order to study the outlandish script on the rim, 'they aren't on the list.'

'What list?'

'The list of stolen gold and silver we get from the police each month. Or did you nick them recently?'

'I didn't steal them,' said Malcolm truthfully, 'they're mine.'

'Tell that to the inspector, chum,' said the jeweller. A burly assistant stood in front of the door, as the jeweller lifted the telephone and started to dial.

'You people never learn,' he said sadly. 'You come in off the street expecting me to buy five grand's worth of gold . . .'

'As much as that?'

'That's the value of the metal. Add a couple of grand for the workmanship, if it's genuine. I expect the owner will be glad to get them back.'

'Oh, that's all right, you can keep them,' Malcolm said, and vanished.

3

As he put the kettle on back in Nether Stowey, Malcolm worked out a way in which he could turn the Nibelung hoard into mastery of the world. First, he would have to find some way of contacting an unscrupulous gold dealer – not too difficult; all he need do would be to request the Tarnhelm, in its travel mode, to take him to an unscrupulous gold dealer's house and there he would be – and sell off a reasonable quantity of gold with no questions asked. With the money thus obtained, he could start buying shares – lots of shares in lots of big companies. Then sell more gold, then buy more shares. Sooner or later, he would flood the gold market, which would be a pity; but by then, he ought to have enough shares to enable him to do without the gold per se. After about a decade of buying as many shares as he could, he would be in a position to start seizing control of major international companies. Through these (and massive corruption) he could in turn gain influence over the Governments of the countries of the free world.

With the free world in his pocket, he could patch up a workable detente with the Communist bloc to the extent that he could start infiltrating them. By a combination of bribery, economic pressure and, where necessary, military force, he could in about thirty-five years gain unseen but effective control of the world, and probably about a hundred ulcers to go with it. It all sounded perfectly horrible and no fun at all, and Malcolm wanted no part of it. In a way he was relieved. Control of the world, as he had imagined it would be when Ingolf first mentioned the subject, would have entailed responsibilities as well as benefits. As it was, he could perfectly well throw the Ring away – back into the Rhine, if the Rhinedaughters had not long since died of sewage poisoning – and keep the Tarnhelm for his own amusement. He could get a job as an express messenger . . .

'Idiot,' said a voice.

He looked round, startled. There was nobody to be seen . . . then he remembered. The voice had come from a rather bedraggled pigeon perched on his window ledge.

'I beg your pardon?' he said.

'You're an idiot, Malcolm Fisher,' said the pigeon. 'Open the window and let me in.'

Although he was beginning to tire of being insulted and ordered about by dumb animals, Malcolm did as he was told.

'Sorry,' said the pigeon, 'it was rude of me. But I felt it was my duty to tell you. You see, I'm a woodbird, like the woodbird who advised Siegfried all those years ago.'

'No, you're not,' said Malcolm. 'You're a pigeon.'

'Correct. I'm a woodpigeon. And we care about things.'

That was presumably meant to be logical. Certainly, it made about as much sense as everything else Malcolm had heard during the past forty-eight hours. 'So why am I an idiot?' he asked. 'What have I done now?'

'The Ring you've got there,' said the pigeon, its beak full of crumbs from Malcolm's table, 'you don't understand what it is, do you? I mean, you've heard the story and you've read the book . . .'

'When do I get to see the film?'

'It's not a toy, you know,' said the pigeon, sternly, 'and before you ask, I know all this because I'm a bird.'

'Thank you.'

'You're welcome. You see,' continued the pigeon, preening its ruffled feathers, 'the Ring has other powers beyond creating wealth that were not even guessed at – good

29

crumbs these, by the way. I'm into healthy scavenging – guessed at when it was forged. Have you heard today's news?'

Malcolm looked at his watch; it was five o'clock, and he leaned forward to switch on the radio. But even before he touched the set, the voice of the newsreader became clearly audible.

'That's handy,' said Malcolm.

'Giant's blood,' replied the pigeon. 'Of course, it's selective; you can only hear the broadcasts if you make a conscious decision to do so. Otherwise you'd go mad in a couple of minutes, with all those voices jabbering away in a hundred different languages. And yes, it does work with telephones.'

'Don't tell me,' said Malcolm, to whom a sudden revelation had been made, 'you birds can do it as well.'

The pigeon did not speak. Nevertheless Malcolm heard it clearly in his mind's ear. Although the bird did not open its beak, it was exactly the same as hearing a voice, rather like having a conversation with someone with their back to you. Even the pigeon's faint Midlands accent was preserved.

'And you can do everything that we can do, as well or even better. For instance you can read thoughts, like you're doing now – selectively, of course. But in your case, you can blot them out and hear nothing if you want to. We can't.'

One distinct advantage of this conversation without speech was that these communications, which would have taken several seconds to say out loud, flashed through Malcolm's mind in no time at all. To give an illustration: an actor reciting the whole of *Paradise Lost* by thought-transfer would detain his audience for no more than six minutes. As Malcolm opened his mind to the concept, he found that he could hear the pigeon's thoughts even when it wasn't trying to communicate them.

'Same to you,' he said (or thought) irritably.

'Sorry,' said the bird. 'I forgot you could hear. That's why we birds never evolved very far, I suppose, despite our considerable intelligence. We have to spend all our time and energy watching what we think, and so we can never get around to using our brains for anything useful. You humans only have to watch what you say. You're lucky.'

'Where was I?'

'Listening to the radio.'

'Oh, yes.'

This entire conversation had taken up the time between the second and third pips of the Greenwich time signal. Malcolm, whose mind had grown used to working at a faster speed, found the wait for the next pip unendurably dull, as whole seconds of inactivity ticked by. When the newsreader started speaking, her words were at first almost incomprehensible, like a recording slowed right down.

The announcer seemed rather harassed, for her beautiful BBC voice was distinctly strained as she went through the catalogue of natural and man-made disasters that had struck the planet since about one o'clock that morning.

'When you killed the Giant,' said the pigeon.

There had been earthquakes all across North and South America, a volcano had erupted in Italy, and a swarm of locusts bigger than any previously recorded had formed over North Africa. Seven Governments had been violently overthrown, the delicate peace negotiations in the Middle East had collapsed, the United States had broken off diplomatic relations with China, and England had lost the First Test by an innings and thirty-two runs.

'That's awful,' said Malcolm, aloud.

'Listen,' urged the pigeon.

Amazingly enough, said the announcer (and her voice palpably quavered) in all these disasters nobody had been killed or even seriously injured, anywhere in the world, although the damage to property had been incalculable. Meanwhile, at London Zoo Za-Za the Giant Panda . . .

31

Malcolm dismissed the voice from his mind. 'So what's going on?'

The pigeon was silent and its mind was blank. 'Is it my fault?' Malcolm demanded impatiently. 'Did I do all that?'

'No, not exactly. In fact, I would say it was sort of a tribute to your integrity, like.'

'My what?'

'Integrity. You see, because of the curse Alberich put on it, the Ring can't help causing destruction. Every day it continues to exist, it exercises power on the world, and unless this power is channelled deliberately into positive and constructive things, which is impossible anyway, it just sort of crashes about, causing damage and breaking things.'

'What sort of things?'

'The earth's crust. Governments. You name it. Why do you think the world's been such a horrible place for the last thousand years? Ingolf couldn't care less what happened to the world so long as he was all right, and over the past century and a bit, when his temper wasn't improved by perpetual toothache, he actively encouraged the Ring by thinking unpleasant thoughts. Hence wars, progress and all the rest of it.'

Malcolm shook his head in disbelief. 'But . . . but what about the Gods, then? I mean, I've only just found out they exist. What do they do?'

'What they like, mostly. Wotan – he's the only one who matters – is omnipotent; well, omnipotent up to a point. The only thing he can't compete with is the Ring, which is far more powerful than he is. That's why he wants it so badly. But it doesn't really interfere with his being all-powerful. You see, no-one can control the Ring, or make it do what they want it to. That's the point . . .'

The pigeon's thought tailed off into a blank. Something had obviously occurred to it that it could not even put into thoughts, let alone words. It made an effort and continued.

'Needless to say,' said the pigeon, 'when the Ring changes hands, it gets very temperamental. Nobody likes being killed, and all the bad vibes that went through Ingolf's mind as he died last night won't have made things any better. You see, bad thoughts give the Ring something to get its teeth into. Hence all those earthquakes.'

Once again, the pigeon's thoughts tailed away. It walked round the table, pecked at a Biro, and then stopped dead in its tracks.

'And nobody got killed,' it said. 'That's strange, don't you think? Did you put the Ring on straight away?'

'Yes.'

'I don't know if this is even possible, but maybe you *were* controlling the Ring in some way or other, stopping it from actually killing anyone. God knows how. I mean, even Siegfried couldn't control it, and he was much more . . .'

'I know, so everyone keeps telling me.'

'Anyway, he couldn't stop the curse, although he was probably the only one so far who had the potential – he was Wotan's grandson, but no longer in his power. But perhaps it's not the curse . . . Anyway, he couldn't do a thing with it. And look at you . . .'

'In that case,' said Malcolm, 'all I have to do to end this whole curse business and make the world safe, all I have to do is throw the Ring back into the Rhine. It was the Rhine, wasn't it?'

The pigeon flapped its wings and flew round the room to relieve its feelings. It didn't work.

'Idiot!' it shouted. 'You haven't been listening to a word I've thought, have you? That's the worst possible thing you could do.'

'But it said in the book: The waters of the Rhine will wash away Alberich's curse.'

'How quaintly you put it, I'm sure. You haven't grasped the point I've been trying to make. The curse isn't like that. In fact . . . Sorry.' The pigeon fluttered up from the table and perched forgivingly on Malcolm's head. 'I forgot, you aren't used to reading thoughts. Only it's just occurred to me that the curse is nothing to do with it. It's just a curse, that's all. It just brings all the owners of the Ring to a horrible and untimely death. But the Ring was powerful *before* Alberich put the curse on it. If you were to throw the Ring into the Rhine . . .'

'Would you please stop pecking at my head?'

'Sorry. It's instinct, I'm afraid. We birds are martyrs to instinct. Where was I? If you were to throw the Ring into the Rhine, there's no guarantee that the Rhinedaughters would be able to control its nasty habits any more than Ingolf could. And even if they could and they wanted to, they can't be expected to be able to guard it properly against the bad guys – Wotan and Alberich and that lot. Let alone any new contenders. They have no power, you see, they can only offer an alternative.'

'What alternative?'

'Think about it.' The pigeon chuckled. 'In the Dark Ages, of course, it was inconceivable that anyone would prefer unlimited wealth to a bit of fun with a pretty Rhinedaughter – that's what all that stuff about forswearing Love was about – but that was a thousand years ago. What could you buy a thousand years ago that was worth having? The ultimate in consumer goods was a rowing-boat or a goatskin hat, and the ideal home was a damp log cabin with no chimney. These days, everything has changed. These days, most people would forswear Love for a new washing-machine, let alone the entire world. No, if you throw the Ring into the Rhine, you'll make everything much worse.'

Malcolm buried his head in his hands, causing the pigeon to lose its balance. 'Watch out,' it said.

'But Wagner said . . .'

'Forget Wagner, this is real life.'

'Where did he get the story from, by the way?'

'A little bird told him.'

Malcolm sat for a moment in silence, while the pigeon tried to eat his diary.

'This is terrible,' he said at last. 'Now I'm going to be

personally responsible for every catastrophe in the world. And I thought it was only my mother who blamed me for everything.'

'Not necessarily,' said the pigeon, soothingly. 'Perhaps – I say perhaps – you can stop all these terrible things from happening. Don't ask me how, but you stopped I don't know how many people from being killed today.'

'Did I?'

'Well, if you didn't, then who the hell did? Let me put it to you this way.' The pigeon buried its beak in its feathers and thought hard for a moment. 'By and large, all things considered, you wouldn't actually want to kill anyone, now would you?'

'No,' replied Malcolm, 'certainly not.'

'But when you hear about disasters in other countries, it doesn't spoil your day. You think, Hard luck, poor devils, but you don't burst out crying all over the place.'

'True.'

'Whereas a disaster in this country would affect you rather more deeply, wouldn't it?'

'Yes, I suppose it would.'

'That follows. All these disasters, you see, happened abroad. The only bit of local disaster was that England lost a cricket match, and the way things are nowadays, that would probably have happened anyway. I remember when I was feeding in the outfield at Edgbaston in nineteen fifty-six . . .'

'Get on with it,' said Malcolm irritably.

'The way I see it,' said the pigeon, picking up a crumb of stale cheese it had previously overlooked, 'the Ring is being guided by your will. A certain number of momentous things have to happen when the Ring changes hands. It's like a volcano: all that force and violence has to go somewhere. But your will protected Britain . . .'

'Do you mind not using that word? It makes it sound like my last will and testament.'

'All right then, you protected Britain, because you care

35

more about it than about other countries. All sub-consciously, of course. And you refused to let the Ring kill anybody, because you instinctively don't approve of people being killed. When you think about it, that's pretty remarkable. Have you got any more of that cheese anywhere?'

Malcolm was rather taken aback. 'You mean I really can make the world do what I want?'

'Not in the way you think. The Ring won't take orders from your *conscious* mind. But you can prevent it from destroying the world, if you're sufficiently strong-minded.'

'But that can't be right.'

'It does seem odd, I agree. After all, Wotan couldn't do it. Fafner couldn't do it. Even Siegfried couldn't do it and he was much more . . .'

'Siegfried was an idiot. Or did Wagner get that wrong, too?'

'Yes, he did. Siegfried wasn't an idiot, not by a long way. He just didn't know what was going on. But then, neither did you.' The pigeon fell silent again.

'How come I can't read your thoughts? Malcolm asked. 'You've done this two or three times now.'

'I'm not so much thinking as communing.'

'What with?'

'How should I know?' snapped the pigeon in a sudden flurry of bad temper. 'Mother Earth, I've always assumed. Go on, you try it.'

Malcolm tried it, opening his mind to everything in the world. There was a perfectly horrible noise and he switched it off. 'Nothing,' he said, 'just a lot of voices.'

'Oh,' said the pigeon, and Malcolm could sense unease, even awe, in its thoughts. 'Oh, I *see*.'

'You mean it's me you're communing with?' Malcolm was so amazed that he turned himself into a stone without intending to.

'That's the way it's looking,' said the pigeon. 'Sir,' it added.

36

'Go ahead,' said Malcolm bitterly. 'You and my Immortal Soul have a nice chat, don't mind me.'

'I'm sorry,' said the pigeon, 'I suppose it must be very frustrating for you, especially since it's so good, you'd enjoy it if you could hear it, you really would.'

'What did it say last?'

'Well, it suggested that you may not be wise or noble or fearless or brave or cunning or anything like that . . .'

'That sounds like me talking.'

'. . . But you're probably the only *nice* person in history to own the wretched thing.'

'Nice?'

'Nice.'

'You really think I'm nice?' said Malcolm, blushing.

'Where I come from,' said the pigeon, 'that's not a compliment. Anyway, I didn't say it, you did, only you couldn't hear yourself think. But if by nice you mean decent, inoffensive, wouldn't hurt a fly, yes, I think you probably are. And all the other Ring-Bearers have been right bastards in one way or another.'

'Even Siegfried?'

'Siegfried had a wicked temper. If his porridge wasn't just right, he'd throw it all round the hall.'

Malcolm rubbed his eyes. 'And my niceness is going to save the world, is it?'

'Could do, who knows? Just try saying to yourself over and over again, I don't want anything bad to happen to anyone anywhere today. See if that makes any difference.' The pigeon turned its head and looked at the sun, which was starting to shine with the evening light. 'Time I was on my way,' it said. 'There's a field of oilseed rape out there I want to look in on as I go home. They've got one of those machines that go bang every ten minutes, but who cares? I like it round here. Always wanted to retire to the seaside.'

'So that's it, is it? Think nice thoughts?'

'Try it. If it doesn't work, try something else. Well, take care, won't you? It's been a privilege meeting you, I suppose. But watch out for the Gods and the Volsungs for a while. They'll be after you by now.'

'Can they read thoughts too?'

'No, but Wotan has a couple of clever ravens. I don't think they can find you easily, though. The Tarnhelm masks your thoughts, except at very short range, and the world's a very big place. You've got the advantage, having the Tarnhelm. But if I were you, I'd be a bit more discreet in future. It's not clever to go around looking like people who have been dead for a thousand years.'

'You mean Theseus?'

'Who's that? No, I mean Siegfried. And Brunnhilde, come to that.' The pigeon flapped its wings, said, 'Thanks for the crumbs,' and was gone.

For a moment, Malcolm did not understand what the pigeon had said about Siegfried and . . . He had only turned himself into one female character today. He stood in front of the mirror.

'Quick,' he ordered, 'Siegfried, then Brunnhilde.'

Once again, the images of the Most Handsome Man and the Most Beautiful Woman flashed across the glass. He sat down on the bed and, for some reason or other, began to cry.

4

Apotheosis can be rather unnerving. Even the most hardened and cynical Royal visitor to remote islands is taken aback to find the islanders worshipping his framed photograph, and he at least has the consolation of knowing that he isn't really a God. Malcolm had no such consolation as he faced up to the fact that his mind controlled the world.

'If only,' he kept on saying to himself, 'Mr Scanlon knew.' Mr Scanlon had tried to teach him Physics at school, and if his assessment of Malcolm's mental capacities had been correct, the world was in deep trouble. For his part, Malcolm had always been inclined to share his teacher's opinion; certainly, the weight of the evidence had always seemed to be on Mr Scanlon's side. Nevertheless, it was necessary to make the best of a bad job. Malcolm now had literally no-one to blame but himself, and the Daily Service on the radio seemed to be directly addressed to him. Especially one line, which Malcolm took it upon himself to paraphrase slightly:

'For there is none other that fighteth for us, but only thou. Oh, *God!*'

But the news from the outside world gave him grounds for cautious optimism. The disasters that had marked his accession cleared themselves up with embarrassing speed. The United Nations, for example, held a special session in New York and unanimously voted to levy an unprecedented contribution from all its members to relieve the suffering of the victims of the catastrophe. The various coups and revolutions resolved themselves into benign democracies as if that had been their intention all along. Peace negotiations in the Middle East were resumed, America and China started playing each other at ping-pong again, and the swarm of locusts was devoured by a huge flock of migrating birds. Admittedly, England lost the Second Test as well, but Malcolm knew that he could not be expected to work miracles. The only disaster that had been reported was the destruction by volcanic forces of a small, uninhabited atoll in the middle of the Pacific Ocean; and even that had its good side, as the residents of the neighbouring atoll had always complained that it was an eyesore and spoilt their view of the sunset.

It needed no ghost come from the grave, and no visitation of prophetic birds to tell Malcolm that this was all the result of being nice. He had rigorously excluded from his mind all unpleasant, spiteful or angry thoughts for the best part of a fortnight (the strain was beginning to show), and the result had been a quite unparalleled upturn in the fortunes of the human race. 'And all that,' Malcolm reflected smugly, 'was me.'

But it was extremely frustrating to have to keep all this to oneself. Malcolm had never achieved anything before, except third prize in a village flower show when he was nine (three people had entered that particular category), and the wish to be congratulated was very strong. His sister, for example, had achieved many things, but she had never stopped a war or disposed of a swarm of locusts. But the Ring seemed to cut him off from the rest of the human race. Although he was the master of the Tarnhelm, he scarcely went out at all. This was partly laziness, partly caution; for if he was to remain nice and keep his mind free of malice or resentment, it would not be advisable for him to see any of his friends or relatives. He was also beginning to feel extremely hungry. All the food lying about the flat (some of which had been there for a considerable time) was long since finished, he had no money left, and he could see little prospect of getting any more. Even if his job still existed (and after two weeks' unexplained absence, that seemed unlikely) he knew that for the sake of mankind he could not go back to it. One cannot work as a clerk in a provincial auction room without entertaining some fairly dark thoughts, any one of which, given his present position, could blot out a major city. The obvious alternative – theft, using the power of the Tarnhelm – was open to the same objection. If he were to start stealing things, who could tell what the consequences might be?

He contemplated the problem, turning himself into Aristotle in the hope that the transformation might assist his powers of reasoning. During the past two weeks, metamorphosis had been virtually his only occupation, and had kept him moderately amused. He had always rather wanted to know what various characters from history and fiction really looked like, especially the girls described by the poets. He also took the trouble to assume the shapes of all his likely assailants – Wotan and Alberich and Loge – so as to be able to recognise them instantly, and had frightened himself half to death in the process.

The outward shape of Aristotle seemed to inspire him, and he went through the various ways in which he could sell gold for money without actually getting involved himself. Having dismissed the notion of putting an advertisement in the Classified section of the *Quantock Gazette*, he hit upon what seemed to be an acceptable notion. Armed with a large suitcase, he commanded the Tarnhelm to take him to some uninhabited vault in the Bank of England where he might find plenty of used banknotes. On arrival, he filled the suitcase (more of a small trunk) with ten- and twenty-pound notes, then started to materialise gold to a roughly equivalent value. By the time he had finished, his forehead was quite sore with rubbing and the floor of the vault was covered in exquisite treasures. He removed himself and the suitcase and tried the equivalent banks in France, America, Australia and other leading countries (for it would be unfair if only one or two countries suddenly found themselves linked to the gold standard). With the immense wealth he gathered in this way, he opened a large number of bank accounts in various names – a terrifying business, full of unforeseen complications – and bought himself the house he had always wanted, a huge and extremely attractive manor house near Taunton, which happened to be for sale.

As he had anticipated, no mention was made by any of the financial institutions with which he had done business of the sudden disappearance of large sums of money or the equally unexpected appearance of a fortune in gold. The price of the metal fluctuated wildly for a day or so, then went considerably higher than it had been for some time. Intrigued, Malcolm revisited his favourite banks, invisible and carrying two suitcases. All the gold had gone, and there were plenty more banknotes, neatly packaged up for ease of transportation. In the national bank of Australia there was even a piece of card with 'Thanks; Please Call Again' written on it, propped up on a shelf.

Now that he was a multi-millionaire on both sides of the Iron Curtain, Malcolm turned his attention to furnishing his new house. It seemed likely that he would have to spend a great deal of time in it, on his own, and since money was no object, he decided to have the very best of everything. It was obvious that he could not risk appearing there in his own shape – what would Malcolm Fisher be doing buying Combe Hall? – and so he designed for himself a new persona to go with his new life. In doing so, he made a terrible mistake; but by the time he realised what he had done, it was too late.

It was simple carelessness on his part that caused the trouble. He had been so excited at the prospect of owning Combe Hall that he had gone to the estate agents who were handling the sale in his own shape. He was shown into an office and asked to wait while the senior partner came down to see him, and as the door opened to admit this gentleman, Malcolm caught sight of his own, original face in the mirror and realised his mistake. He commanded the

Tarnhelm to change him into someone else, but did not have time to specify who. To his horror, he saw that the face in the mirror was that of the Most Handsome Man; but the estate agent had seen him now, so he could not change into anything less conspicuous. He had stuck like it, just as his mother had warned him he would.

Thus it was that Malcolm found himself condemned to embark on his new life with the face and body of Siegfried the Dragon-Slayer, also known as the Most Handsome Man. He could not help remembering the pigeon's warning about this, but it was too late now. Not that Malcolm objected in principle to being the most handsome man who had ever lived; but the sight of ravens (or crows, or blackbirds; he was no ornithologist) filled him with horror.

Meanwhile, he fleshed out his new character and by deviousness and contrivance of which he had not thought himself capable acquired the necessary documents and paperwork. In order to give his new self a history (multi-millionaires do not simply appear from nowhere) he had to Tarnhelm himself at dead of night into the computer rooms of half the public records offices in the country, and since he knew next to nothing about twentieth-century machines, he accidentally erased the life histories of several hundred people before getting the result he wanted. Finally, however, he ended up with everything he needed to be Herr Manfred Finger of Düsseldorf, the name and identity he had chosen. Again, the German aspect was ill-advised and unintentional; he had wanted to be a foreigner of some sort (since in Somerset it is understood that all foreigners are mad, and allowances for eccentric or unusual behaviour are made accordingly) and had chosen a country at random. That he should have chosen Germany was either yet more carelessness or else the Ring trying to get its own back on him for making it do good in the world. He was not sure which, but was inclined to the first explanation, as being more in keeping with his own nature.

Herr Finger was soon familiar to all the inhabitants of

Combe, who were naturally curious to know more about their new neighbour. As local custom demanded, they soon found a nickname for the new Lord of the Manor. The various members of the Booth family who had owned the Hall from the early Tudor period onwards had all been known by a variety of affectionate epithets – Mad Jack, or Drunken George – and the periphrasis bestowed on Malcolm was 'that rich foreign bastard'. Such familiarity did not, however, imply acceptance. Although it was generally admitted that Herr Finger was not too bad on the surface and no worse than the last of the Booths (Sir William, or Daft Billy), it went without saying that there was something wrong about him. He was, it was agreed, a criminal of some sort; but whether he was an illegal arms dealer or a drug smuggler, the sages of Combe could not be certain. The only thing on which everyone was unanimous was that he had murdered his wife. After all, none of them had ever seen her in the village . . .

'And what time,' said Wotan, 'do you call this?'

Loge, his hands covered in oil, climbed wearily off his motorcycle and removed his helmet. 'It broke down again,' he said. 'Just outside Wuppertal. Plugs.'

Wotan shook his head sadly. Admittedly, it had been on his orders that the immortal Gods had traded in their eight-legged horses and chariots drawn by winged cats for forms of transport more suited to the twentieth century, but he expected his subordinates to be both punctual and properly turned out. Cleanliness, he was fond of asserting, is next to godliness.

'Well, you're here now,' he said. 'So what do you make of *that*?'

Loge looked about him. There was nothing to see except corn-fields. He said so.

'Well done,' growled Wotan. 'We are unusually observant this morning, are we not? And what do you find unusual about the corn in these corn-fields?'

Loge scratched his head, getting oil on his hair. 'Dunno,' he said. 'It looks perfectly normal to me.'

'Normal for August?'

'Perfectly.'

'It's June.'

Loge, who had spent an hour wrestling with a motorcycle engine beside a busy autobahn, did not at first appreciate the significance of this remark. Then the pfennig dropped. 'It's two months in advance, you mean?'

'Precisely.' Wotan put his arm around Loge's shoulder. 'Good, wouldn't you say?'

'I suppose so.'

'It's bloody marvellous, considering the weather they've been having this year. And why do you suppose the crops are doing so very, very well? In fact, why is everything in the world doing so very, very well? Answer me that?'

Loge instinctively looked up at the sky. Thunder-clouds were beginning to form.

'Someone's been interfering?' he suggested.

'Correct!' Wotan shouted, and the first clap of thunder came in, dead on cue. 'Someone's been interfering. Now who could that be? Who on earth could be responsible for this new golden age?'

From his tone, Loge guessed that it couldn't have been Wotan himself. Which left only one candidate. 'You mean the Ring-Bearer?'

'Very good. The only force in the Universe capable of making things happen so quickly and so thoroughly. But isn't that a trifle strange in itself? Wouldn't you expect the Ring to do nasty things, not nice ones? Left to itself, I mean?'

Loge agreed that he would.

'So you would agree that anyone capable of making the Ring do what it doesn't want to do is likely to be a rather special person?'

Wotan had picked up this irritating habit of asking leading questions from the late and unlamented Socrates. Loge hated it.

'In fact, someone so remarkable that even if he didn't have the Ring he would present a serious danger to our security. And since he does have the Ring . . .'

Wotan was trembling with rage, and the rain was falling fast, beating down the standing corn. 'We have to find him, quickly,' he roared. 'Otherwise, we are in grave danger. To be precise, *you* have to find him. Do you understand?'

Loge understood, but Wotan wanted to make his point. 'And if I were you, my friend, I would spare no effort in looking for him. I would leave no stone unturned and no avenue unexplored. And do you know why? Because if you don't, you might very well find yourself spending the rest of Eternity as a waterfall. You wouldn't like that, now would you?'

Loge agreed that he wouldn't, and Wotan was about to develop this theme further when it stopped raining. The clouds dispersed, and the sun shone brightly, pitching a vivid rainbow across the blue sky.

'Who said you could stop raining?' screamed Wotan. 'I want lightning. Now!'

The sky took no notice, and Loge went white with fear. Everyone has his own particular phobia, and Loge was terrified of fish. As a waterfall, he would have salmon jumping up him all day long. He would have prayed for rain if he wasn't a God himself. But the sky remained cloudless.

'That does it!' Wotan smashed his fist into the palm of his left hand. 'When I'm not even allowed to rain my own rain because it damages the crops, it's time for positive action.' He stood still for a moment, then turned to Loge.

'Are you still here?' he asked savagely.

'I'm on my way,' Loge replied, jumping desperately on the kickstart of his motorcycle. 'I'll find him, don't you worry.'

Loge sped off into the distance, and Wotan was left alone, staring angrily at the sun. Two coal-black ravens floated down and settled on the fence.

'Nice weather we're having,' said Thought.

For some reason, this did not go down well. 'Any result?' Wotan snapped.

'Nothing so far, boss,' said Memory.

'Where have you been looking?'

'Everywhere, boss. But you know we can't find the Ring-Bearer. We can't see him, or read his thoughts, or anything like that.'

'God give me strength!' Wotan clenched his fist and made an effort to relax. 'Then what you do, you stupid bird, is go through all the people of the world, one by one, and when you find one whose thoughts you can't read and who you can't see, that's him. I'd have thought that was obvious.'

Thought looked at Memory. Memory looked at Thought. 'But that'll take weeks, boss,' said Memory.

'So what else were you planning to do?'

The two ravens flapped their wings and launched themselves into the air. They circled for a moment, then floated over the world. All day they flew, sweeping in wide circles across the continents, until Memory suddenly swooped down and landed beside the banks of the Rhine.

'Stuff this,' he said to Thought. 'Why don't we ask the girls?'

'Good idea,' said Memory. 'Wish I'd thought of that.'

'It must have slipped your mind.' The two birds took off again, but this time they flew only a mile or so, to a spot where, about a thousand years ago, a certain Alberich had stopped and watched three beautiful women swimming in the river. The ravens landed in a withered tree and folded their wings.

Under the tree, three young girls were sunbathing, and for them the Sun Goddess had saved the best of the evening

47

light, for she was their friend.

'Flosshilde,' said one of the girls, 'there's a raven in that tree looking at you.'

'I hope he likes what he sees,' replied the Rhinedaughter lazily.

Wellgunde, the eldest and most serious of the three, rolled onto her stomach and lifted her designer sunglasses.

'Hello, Thought,' she said, 'hello, Memory. Found him yet, then?'

The ravens were silent, ruffling their coarse feathers with their beaks, and the girls giggled.

'But you've been looking for simply ages,' said Woglinde, the youngest and most frivolous of the three. 'It must be *somewhere*.'

'I'm always losing things,' said Flosshilde. 'Where do you last remember seeing it?'

'You sure it's not in your pocket?'

'You've put it somewhere safe and you can't remember where?'

Wotan's ravens had been putting up with this sort of thing for a thousand years, but it still irritated them. The girls laughed again, and Memory blushed under his feathers.

'If you don't find him soon,' yawned Flosshilde, combing her long, golden hair, 'he'll slip through your claws, just like clever old Ingolf did. By the way, fancy Ingolf being a badger!'

'He'll get the hang of the Tarnhelm and then no-one will ever find him,' purred Woglinde. 'What a shame that would be.'

'Good luck to him,' said Wellgunde. 'Who wants the boring old Ring, anyway?'

'Dunno what you're being so bloody funny about,' said Memory. 'Supposed to be your Ring we're looking for.'

'Forget it,' said Woglinde, waving her slender arms. 'It's a lovely day, the sun is shining, the crops are growing . . .'

Memory winced at this. Flosshilde giggled.

'. . . And it's been so long since Alberich took the beastly thing that we don't really care any more, do we?' Woglinde wiggled her toes attractively, in a way that had suggested something far nicer than measureless wealth for thousands of years. 'What do we want with gold when we have you to entertain us?'

'Save it for the human beings,' said Memory.

'I wonder what he looks like,' said Wellgunde. 'I bet you he's handsome.'

'And strong.'

'And noble. Don't forget noble.'

'I never could resist noble,' said Woglinde, watching the ravens carefully under her beautiful eyelashes.

'We came to tell you that we'd heard something,' said Thought. 'But since you're not interested any more . . .'

Wellgunde yawned, putting her hand daintily in front of her mouth. 'You're right,' she said. 'We're not.' She turned over onto her back and picked up a magazine.

'Something interesting, we've heard,' said Memory.

'Oh, all right,' said Flosshilde, smiling her most dazzling smile. 'Tell us if you must.'

Even Wotan's ravens, who are (firstly) immortal and (secondly) birds, cannot do much against the smiles of Rhinedaughters. But since Memory was bluffing, there was nothing for him to do.

'I didn't say we were going to tell you what we'd heard,' he said, archly, 'only that we'd heard it.' It is not easy for a raven to be arch, but Memory had been practising.

'Oh go away,' said Flosshilde, throwing a piece of orange peel at the two messengers. 'You're teasing us, as usual.'

'You wait and see,' said Memory, lamely, but the three girls jumped up and dived into the water, as elegantly as the very best dolphins.

'We know something you don't know,' chanted Flosshilde, and the Sun-Goddess made the water sparkle around her floating hair. Then she disappeared, leaving behind only a stream of silver bubbles.

'I dunno,' said Thought. 'Women.'

The ravens flapped their heavy wings, circled morosely for a while, and flew away.

By a strange coincidence, a few moments after Flosshilde dived down to the bed of the Rhine, three identical girls hopped out of the muddy, fetid waters of the River Tone, at the point where it runs through the centre of Taunton. A few passers-by stopped and stared, for the three girls were far cleaner than anyone who has recently had anything to do with the Tone has any right to be. But the girls' smiles wiped such thoughts from their minds, and they went on their way whistling and wishing that they were twenty years younger. Had they realised that what they had just seen were the three Rhinedaughters, Flosshilde, Well-gunde and Woglinde, they might perhaps have taken a little more notice.

5

One of the things that slightly worried Malcolm was the fact that he was becoming decidedly middle-aged. For example, the ritualised drinking of afternoon tea had come to mean a lot to him, not simply because it disposed of an hour's worth of daylight. He had chosen half-past four in the afternoon as the best time for reading the daily papers, and from half-past four to half-past five (occasionally a quarter to six) each day he almost made himself feel that he enjoyed being extremely nice and bored stiff, for he knew that all the good news that filled the papers was, in one way or another, his doing.

Today, there was any amount of good news from around the world. Malcolm could sense the frustration and despair of the editors and journalists as they forced themselves to report yet more bumper harvests, international accords and miraculous cures. Admittedly, there had been a freak storm in Germany (banner headlines in the tabloids) and some crops had been damaged in a few remote areas. Nevertheless, he noted with satisfaction, this minor disaster was not entirely a bad thing, since it had prompted the EEC to draft and sign a new agreement on compensating farmers for damage caused by acts of God. So every cloud, however small, had a silver lining, although these days it was beginning to look as though only a very few silver linings had clouds.

Malcolm tried to work out what could have caused the freak storm in the first place. He picked up the *Daily Mirror* ('German farmers in rain horror') and observed that the storm had started at three o'clock their time, which was two o'clock our time, which was when Malcolm's new secretary had finally managed to corner him and force him to sign five letters. He resolved to be more patient with her in future, and not call her a whatsisname under his breath.

His tea was stone cold, but that did not matter; it was, after all, Only Him. That was a marvellous phrase, and one that he had come to treasure. When one has suddenly been forced into the role of the Man of Sorrows, self-pity is the only luxury that remains. In fact, Malcolm had no objection whatsoever to taking away the sins of the world, but it was useful to keep an option on self-pity just in case it came in useful later. He poured the cold tea onto the lawn and watched it soak into the ground. In the crab-apple tree behind him, a robin perched and sang excitedly, but he ignored it, closing his mind to its persistent chirping. He had found that the little birds liked to come up to him and confide their secrets that they could not share with other birds, and at first he had found this extremely flattering. But since the majority of these confidences were extremely personal and of interest only to a trained biologist, he had decided that it would be best not to encourage them. After a while, the robin stopped singing and went away. Malcolm rose to his feet and walked slowly into the house.

Combe Hall was undoubtedly very beautiful, but it was also very big. It had been built in the days when a house-holder tended to feel claustrophobic if he could not accommodate at least one infantry regiment, including the band, in his country house. Its front pediment was world famous. Its windows had been praised and reviled in countless television series. Its kitchens were enormous and capable of being put to any use except the convenient preparation of food. It was very grand, very magnificent, and very empty.

Malcolm had always fancied living at Combe Hall on the strict understanding that his wish was never to come true. Now that he was its owner and (apart from the legion of staff) its only resident, he felt rather like a bewildered traveller at an international airport. The house was bad enough, but the staff were truly awful. There was no suave, articulate butler and no pretty parlourmaids; instead, Malcolm found himself employing an army of grimly professional contract cleaners and an incomprehensible Puerto Rican cook, whom he was sure he was shamelessly exploiting in some way he could not exactly understand. After a week, Malcolm left them all to it and retreated to one of the upstairs drawing-rooms, which he turned into a nicely squalid bedsit.

As a result, he felt under no obligation to assume the role of country gentleman. With the house had come an enormous park, some rather attractive gardens, into which Malcolm hardly dared go for fear of offending the gardeners, and the Home Farm. Ever since he could remember, Malcolm had listened to the Archers on the radio – not from choice, but because they had always been there in his childhood, and so had become surrogate relatives – and his mental picture of agriculture had been shaped by this influence. But the farm that he owned (now *there* was a thought!) whirred and purred with machines and clicked and ticked with computers, filling its owner with fear and amazement. Yet when he suggested to the farm manager that the whole thing might perhaps be rearranged on more picturesque lines and to hell with the profits, which nobody really needed, the farm manager stared at him as if he were mad. Since then, he had kept well away from it.

But with his new property came certain ineluctable responsibilities, the most arduous of which was coping with his new secretary. On the one hand, the woman was invaluable, for she ran the place and left him alone for most of the time. Without the irritations and petty nuisances of everyday life to contend with, he could keep his temper and make the maize grow tall all over Africa. But for this freedom from care he had to pay a severe price: his secretary, who was American and in her middle forties, had clearly made a resolution to be more English than anyone else in the history of the world. Her convert's passion for all things English gave her the zeal of a missionary, and it was obvious that she intended to Anglicise young Herr Finger if it killed her. And, like many missionaries, she was not above a little persecution in the cause of the communication of Enlightenment.

Apart from avoiding his staff and his secretary and anything else that might tend to irritate or annoy, however, Malcolm found that he had very little to do. Even as a small boy, he had never had a hobby of any kind, and he had always found making friends as difficult as doing jigsaw puzzles, and even less rewarding. As for the comfort and solace of his family, Malcolm knew only too well that that was out of the question. If, by some miracle, he could persuade his kin to believe this ludicrous tale of rings and badgers, he knew without having to think about it what their reaction would be. 'Malcolm,' his mother would say, 'give that ring back to Bridget *this instant*' – the implication being that it had been meant for her all along.

Not that the possibility had not crossed his mind. Surely, he had reflected, his talented and universally praised sister would make a far better job of all this than he would; she had five A-levels and had been to Warwick University. But somehow he felt sure that Bridget was not the right person for the job. For a start, she did not suffer fools gladly, and since a large percentage of the people of the world are fools, it was possible that she might not give them the care and consideration they needed. Throughout its history, Malcolm reflected, the Ring had been in the possession of gifted, talented, exceptional people, and look what had happened . . .

One morning, when Malcolm was listening (rather proudly) to the morning news, the English Rose, as he had mentally christened her, came hammering on his door. She seemed to have an uncanny knack of knowing where he was.

54

She informed him that the annual Combe Show was to be held in the grounds of the Hall in a fortnight's time. Malcolm, who loathed all such occasions from the bottom of his heart, tried to protest, but without success.

'Oh, but I've been talking to the folks from the village, and they all say that it's the social event of the year,' buzzed the Rose. 'It's one of the oldest surviving fairs in the country. According to the records I consulted . . .'

Malcolm saw that there was no hope of escape. His secretary, apart from having the persistence of a small child in pursuit of chocolate, was an outstanding example of true Ancestor Worship (although it was not her own ancestors that she worshipped; her name was Weinburger) and anything remotely traditional went to her head like wine. In fact, Malcolm was convinced, if she could revive the burning of witches, with all its attendant seventeenth-century pageantry, she probably would.

'But will it not be – how is it in English? – a great nuisance to arrange?' he suggested. That was, of course, the wrong thing to say. The Rose thrived on challenges.

'Herr Finger,' she said, looking at him belligerently over the top of her spectacles, 'that is not my attitude and well you know it. It will be truly rewarding for me to make all the necessary social arrangements for the proposed event, and Mr Ayres, who is the Chairman of the Show Committee, will be calling on you to discuss all the practicalities. There will be the usual livestock competition, of course, and I presume that the equestrian events will follow their customary pattern. I had hoped that we might prevail upon the Committee to revive the Jacobean Sheriff's Races, but Mr Ayres has, at my request, performed a feasibility study and feels that such a revival could not be satisfactorily arranged in the limited space of time left to us before the Show. So I fear that we will have to content ourselves with a gymkhana situation . . .'

Although Malcolm had acquired the gift of tongues from the blood of the Giant, he still had occasional difficulty in understanding his secretary's English. The name Ayres, however, was immediately recognisable. It was a name he was only too familiar with; indeed, he knew virtually all the words in the language that rhymed with it, for Liz Ayres was the girl he loved. Mr William Ayres, the Chairman of the Show Committee, was her father, and a nastier piece of work never read a Massey-Ferguson catalogue. But thoughts of malice or resentment were no longer available to Malcolm, and so finally he agreed. The English Rose scuttled away, no doubt to flick through Debrett (after Sir Walter Elliot, she was its most enthusiastic reader) and Malcolm resigned himself to another meeting with possibly his least favourite person in the world.

William Ayres could trace his ancestry back to the early fifteenth century; his namesake had won the respect of his betters at the battle of Agincourt by throwing down his longbow and pulling a fully armed French knight off his horse with his bare hands. The present William Ayres undoubtedly had the physical strength to emulate his ancestor's deed and, given his unbounded ferocity, would probably relish the opportunity to try. So massively built was he that people who met him for the first time often wondered why he bothered with tractors and the like on his sprawling farm at the top of the valley. Surely he could save both time and money by drawing the plough himself, if necessary with his teeth. Compared to his two sons, however, Mr Ayres was a puny but sunny-tempered dwarf, and Malcolm could at least console himself with the reflection that he would not be confronted with Joe or Mike Ayres at this unpleasant interview.

Malcolm decided that in order to face Mr Ayres it would be necessary for him to be extremely German, for his antagonist had strong views about rich foreigners who bought up fine old houses in England.

'It's a tremendously important occasion,' said Mr Ayres, 'one of the high points of the year in these parts. It's been going on for as long as I can remember, certainly. When Colonel Booth still had the Hall . . .'

Mr Ayres was a widower, and Malcolm toyed with the idea of introducing him to the English Rose. They would have so much in common . . .

'I am most keen on your English traditions, *naturlich*. Let us hope that we can make this a show to be remembered.'

Mr Ayres winced slightly. He disliked the German race, probably because they had thoughtlessly capitulated before he had been old enough to get at them during the War.

'Then perhaps you would care to invite some of the local people to the Hall,' he replied. 'It would be a splendid opportunity for you to get to know your neighbours.'

'Delighted, *das ist sehr gut*.' Mr Ayres did not like the German language, either. '*Aber* – who shall I invite? I am not yet well acquainted with the local folk.'

'Leave that to me,' said Mr Ayres. 'I'll send you a list, if you like.' He drank his tea brutally – everything he did, he seemed to do brutally. 'It should be a good show this year, especially the gymkhana.'

'What is gymkhana?' Malcolm asked innocently. 'In my country we have no such word.'

'So I believe,' said Mr Ayres, who had suspected as much from the start. He did his best to explain, but it was not easy; anyone would have difficulty in explaining such a basic and fundamental concept, just as it would be difficult to explain the sun to a blind man. In the end, he was forced to give up the struggle.

'I'll get my daughter to explain it to you,' he said brightly. 'She and her fiancé – they haven't announced it yet, but it'll be any day now – I expect they'll be taking part in the main competition. And far be it from me, but I think they're in with a good chance. Well, not Liz perhaps, but young Wilcox – that's her fiancé . . .'

Malcolm fought hard to retain his composure, and as he

struggled, slight earth tremors were recorded in California. For all that he had never expected anything to come of his great love for Elizabeth Ayres, the news that she was soon to be engaged and married made him want to break something. Fortunately for the inhabitants of San Francisco he managed to get a grip on himself.

'Ah, that is good,' he said mildly. 'So you will make the necessary arrangements with my secretary, yes? So charmed to have met you. *Auf Wiedersehen.*'

'Good day, Mr Finger.' Mr Ayres stood up, for a moment blotting out the sun, and extended an enormous hand. Malcolm cringed as he met it with his own; he had shaken hands with Mr Ayres once before, and was convinced that the farmer's awesome grip had broken a small bone somewhere. To his surprise, however, he was able to meet the grip firmly and without serious injury, and he suddenly realised that his arm – the arm of Siegfried the Dragon-Slayer, give or take a bit – was as strong or possibly stronger. This made him feel a little better, but not much.

As soon as Mr Ayres had gone, Malcolm sat down heavily and relieved his feelings by tearing up a newspaper. They hadn't announced it yet, but it would be any day now. Soon there would be a coy paragraph in the local paper, followed by a ceremony at the beautiful church with the possibly Saxon font: then a reception at the Blue Boar – the car park full of Range-Rovers, champagne flowing freely (just this once) and minced-up fish on tiny biscuits – and so the line of the bowman of Agincourt would force its way on into the twenty-first century.

Fortune, Malcolm suddenly remembered, can make vile things precious. Like all her family, Liz was obsessed with horses. It might yet be a gymkhana to remember.

When the day came the drive of Combe Hall resembled a plush armoured column, so crowded was it with luxury four-wheel drive vehicles. Large women in hats and large men in blazers, most of whom Malcolm had last seen making nuisances of themselves at the auction rooms in Taunton, strolled through the garden, apparently oblivious of the scowls of the gardeners, or peered through the windows of the house to see what atrocities its new, foreign owner had perpetrated. Malcolm, dressed impeccably and entirely unsuitably in a dark grey suit and crocodile shoes (courtesy of the Tarnhelm; Vorsprung durch Technik, as they say on the Rhine) was making the best job he could of being the shy, charming host, while the English Rose was having the time of her life introducing him to the local gentry. He had provided (rather generously, he thought) a cold collation on the lawn for all the guests on Mr Ayres' list, which they had devoured down to the last sprig of parsley, apparently unaware of the maxim that there is no free lunch.

When the last strand of flesh had been stripped off the last chicken leg, the guests swept like a tweed river into the Park, where the Show was in full swing. A talentless band made up of nasty old men and surly children were playing loudly, but not loudly enough to drown the high-pitched gabble of the Quality, as deafening and intimidating as the buzzing of angry bees. There were innumerable over-weight farm animals in pens, inane sideshows, vintage traction engines, and a flock of sheep, who politely but firmly ignored the efforts of a number of sheepdogs to make them do illogical things. All as it should be, of course, and the centrepiece of this idyll was the show-jumping.

As he surveyed his gentry-mottled grounds, Malcolm was ambushed by the Ayres clan: William, Michael, Joseph, and, of course, Elizabeth. He was introduced to the two terrifying brothers, who rarely made any sound in the presence of their father, and to the daughter of the family. A beautiful girl, Miss Ayres; about five feet three, light brown hair, very blue eyes and a smile you could read small print by. Malcolm, whose mind controlled the world, smiled back, displaying the Dragon-Slayer's geometrically perfect teeth. The two brightest smiles in the world, more dazzling than any toothpaste advertisement, and all this for politeness' sake. Malcolm managed to stop himself shouting, 'Look, Liz, it's me, only much better-looking', and listened attentively as the girl he loved desperately in his nebulous but whole-hearted way explained to him, as by rote, the principles of the gymkhana. To this explanation Malcolm did not listen, for he was using the power he had gained by drinking Giant's blood to read her thoughts. It was easily done and, with the exception of one or two of his school reports, Malcolm had never read anything so discouraging. For although the Tarnhelm had made him the most handsome man in the world, it was evident that Miss Ayres did not judge by appearances. For Liz was wondering who this boring foreigner reminded her of. Now, who was it? Ah, yes. That Malcolm Fisher . . .

He smiled, wished the family good luck in the arena, and walked swiftly away. When he was sure no-one was watching, he turned himself into an appletree and stood for a moment in one of his own hedges, secure in the knowledge that apple trees cannot weep. But even apple trees can have malicious thoughts (ask any botanist) and if the consequences for the world were unfortunate, then so be it. One of Malcolm's few remaining illusions had been shattered: he had always believed that his total lack of attractiveness to the opposite sex was due simply to his unprepossessing appearance, a shortcoming (as he argued) that was in no respect his fault, so that his failure in this field of human endeavour reflected badly not on him but on those who chose to make such shallow and superficial judgements.

The natural consequence of the destruction of this illusion was that Malcolm wanted very much to do something nasty and spiteful, and he wanted to do it to Philip Wilcox, preferably in front of a large number of malicious people. He shrugged his branches, dislodging a blackbird, and resumed his human shape.

Thanks to the blood of the Giant Ingolf, Malcolm could understand all languages and forms of speech, even the curious noises coming out of the tannoy. The competitors in the main event were being asked to assemble in the collecting ring. With the firm intention of turning himself into a horse-fly and stinging Philip Wilcox's horse at an appropriate moment, Malcolm made his way over to the arcade of horseboxes that formed a temporary mews under the shade of a little copse in the west corner of the Park. He recognised the Wilcox family horsebox, which was drawn up at the end of the row. There was the horse, just standing there.

An idea, sent no doubt by the Lord of the Flies, suddenly came into Malcolm's mind. How would it be if . . .? No-one was watching; the attention of the whole world seemed to be focused on a fat child in jodhpurs and his long-suffering pony. Malcolm made himself invisible, and with extreme apprehension (for he was terrified of horses) he led Philip Wilcox's steed out of its box and into the depths of the tangled copse, where he tied it securely to a tree. Then, with his nails pressed hard into the palms of his hands, he changed himself into an exact copy of the animal and transported himself back to the horsebox. This would be hard work, but never mind.

'And have you met the new owner?' asked Aunt Marjorie, settling herself comfortably on a straw bale. 'I never thought I'd live to see the day when a foreigner . . .'

'Just for a few minutes,' replied Liz Ayres. She had learnt over the years the art of separating the questions from the comments in her aunt's conversation, and slipping in answers to them during pauses for breath and other interruptions.

'What's he like? The trouble with most Germans . . .'

'I don't know. He seemed pleasant enough, in a gormless sort of way, but I only said a few words to him.'

'Well, I suppose we should all be very grateful to him for

letting us put a water-jump in the middle of his Park, not that I imagine he minds anyway, or he wouldn't have. Colonel Booth never let us have one, but he was just plain difficult at times. I remember . . .'

'I don't think he's terribly interested in the Hall, actually.' Liz wondered if Aunt Marjorie had ever finished a sentence of her own free will in her life. Probably not. 'I'm told he doesn't *do* anything, just stays indoors all day. Daddy said . . . oh look, there's Joe.'

Elizabeth Ayres' loyalties were sadly divided in the jump-off for the main event, since the two competitors most likely to win it were her brother Joe and her fiancé. Joe was the better rider, but Philip's horse seemed to have found remarkable form just at the right moment. Only last week, Philip had been talking of selling it; perhaps it had been listening (at times, they seem almost human) for today it was sailing over the jumps like a Harrier. Even Aunt Marjorie, who in matters of showjumping was a firm believer in entropy, had admitted that the animal wasn't too bad.

'My money's on your boyfriend,' said Aunt Marjorie. 'What's that horse of his called? It's playing a blinder today. Almost as if it *understood*.'

She had a point there. Intelligence, so Philip had always maintained, had never been one of old Mayfair's attributes. Any animal capable of taking a paper bag or a rusting Mini for a pack of wolves and acting accordingly was unlikely ever to win Mastermind, and this lack of mental as opposed to physical agility had prompted one of Philip's brightest sayings. Even if you led Mayfair to water, he would say, it probably wouldn't even occur to him to drink. But today, Mayfair hadn't put a foot wrong, in any sense.

'Mr Joseph Ayres and Moonbeam,' said the tannoy. A hush fell over the crowd, for it seemed wrong that Joe should be riding the horse instead of the other way round. Joe was obviously the stronger of the two, just as Moonbeam was clearly the more intelligent. Aunt Marjorie, who was, like so many of her class, a sort of refined

Centaur, leaned forward and fixed her round, bright eyes on horse and rider. 'Look at his knees,' she muttered. 'Just *look* at them.'

Joe did his best, but the consensus of opinion was that his best was not going to be good enough. 'Twelve faults,' said the tannoy, and Aunt Marjorie shook her head sadly. 'Why wasn't the idiot using a martingale?' she said. 'When I was a girl . . .'

'Excuse me,' said one of the three rather pretty girls who had just made their way to the front. 'You obviously know all about this sort of thing. Could you tell us what's going on? We're terribly ignorant about horse-racing.'

'It isn't racing, it's jumping,' said Aunt Marjorie, not looking round.

'Oh,' said the youngest of the three girls. 'Oh I *see*.'

'Haven't you been to a show before?' Liz asked, kindly.

'No,' chorused the girls, and this was true. There are no shows and very few gymkhanas at the bottom of the River Rhine, where these three girls, the Rhinedaughters Flosshilde, Wellgunde, and Woglinde, had spent the last two thousand years. They have trout races, but that is not quite the same.

'Well,' said Aunt Marjorie patiently, as if explaining to a Trobriand Islander how to use a fork, 'the idea is to make the horse jump over all the obstacles.'

'Why?' asked Flosshilde. Woglinde scowled at her.

'Because if you don't, you get faults,' said Aunt Marjorie, 'and if you get more faults than everyone else, you lose.'

'That explains a great deal,' said Flosshilde, brightly. 'Thank you.'

'Mr Philip Wilcox on Mayfair,' said the tannoy.

Aunt Marjorie turned to the Rhinemaidens, who were amusing themselves by making atrocious puns on the word 'fault'. 'Watch this,' she urged them. 'He's very good.'

The Rhinedaughters put on their most serious expressions (which were not very serious, in absolute terms) and paid the strictest attention as Philip Wilcox and his tired but determined horse entered the ring. As the horse went past

63

her, Flosshilde suddenly started forward, but Wellgunde nudged her and she composed herself.

'You see,' said Aunt Marjorie, 'he's building up his speed nicely, he's timed it just right, and – oh.'

'Why's he stopped?' asked Woglinde. 'I thought you said he was going to jump over that fence thing.'

Aunt Marjorie, raising her voice above the gasps and whispers of the spectators, explained that that was called a refusal.

'Does he lose marks for that?'

'Yes,' said Liz, crisply.

'He's still got points in hand,' said Aunt Marjorie, trying to stay calm in this crisis. 'I expect he'll go round the other way now. Yes, I thought he would.'

'He's stopped again,' said Woglinde.

'So he has,' said Liz. 'I wonder why?'

'Is he allowed to hit his horse with that stick?' asked Flosshilde. 'It must hurt an awful lot.'

'I think it's cruel,' said Wellgunde.

'I think he's going to try the gate this time,' said Aunt Marjorie nervously. 'Oh dear, not *again* . . .'

'I think it's his fault for hitting the horse with that stick,' said Wellgunde. 'If I was the horse, I'd throw him off.'

'Thirty-three faults,' sniggered the tannoy.

'Is that a lot?' asked Flosshilde. Aunt Marjorie confirmed that it was, rather.

Philip Wilcox was obviously finding it hard to think straight through the buzz of malicious giggling that welled up all around him. About the only jump he hadn't tried yet was the water-jump. He pulled Mayfair's head round, promised him an apple if he made it and the glue factory if he didn't, and pressed with his heels in the approved manner. Mayfair began to move smoothly, rhythmically towards the obstacle.

'Come on, now,' Aunt Marjorie hissed under her breath, 'plenty of pace. Go on . . .'

There is nothing, nothing in the world that amuses human beings more than the sight of a fully grown, fully clothed man falling into water, and sooner or later the human race must come to terms with this fact. But, to the Rhinedaughters (who are not human, but were created by a unique and entirely accidental fusion of the life-forces) it seemed strange that this unfortunate accident should produce such gales of laughter from everyone present, including the tannoy. Even Wellgunde, who thought it served him right for hitting the horse with the stick, was moved to compassion. She looked round to see if she was the only person not laughing, and observed that at least the girl sitting next to the fat woman did not seem to be amused. In fact, she appeared to be perfectly calm, and her face was a picture of tranquillity, like some Renaissance Madonna. Perhaps, thought the Rhinedaughter, she's an immortal too. Or perhaps she's just annoyed.

'I'm so glad Joe won in the end,' said Liz, getting to her feet. 'Shall we go and find some tea?'

Restored to human shape once more, Malcolm crawled into the house and collapsed into a chair. He was utterly exhausted, his mouth was bruised and swollen, his back and sides were aching, and he had pulled a muscle in his neck when he had stopped so suddenly in front of the water-jump. The whole thing had probably hurt him just as much as it had hurt Philip Wilcox, and he had a terrible feeling that it hadn't been worth it. A minute or so of unbridled malice on his part was probably the worst thing that could happen to the universe, and his original argument, that anything that humiliated Philip Wilcox was bound to be good for the world, seemed rather flimsy in retrospect. He could only hope that the consequences would not be too dire.

With an effort, he rose to his feet and stumbled out into the grounds. The show was, mercifully, drawing to a close and, within an hour or so, all the cars that were hiding his grass from the sun would be winding their way home, probably, since this was Somerset, at fifteen miles an hour behind a milk tanker. All he had to do now was present the prizes. This would, of course, mean standing up in public and saying something coherent, and for a moment he stopped dead in his tracks. He should be feeling unmitigated terror at the prospect of this ordeal, but he wasn't. He tried to feel frightened, but the expected reaction refused to materialise. He raised his eyebrows and said 'Well, I'm damned' to himself several times.

As he stood on the platform handing out rosettes, the three Rhinedaughters studied him carefully through their designer sunglasses.

'No, don't tell me,' whispered Flosshilde, 'I'll remember in a minute.'

'Siegfried,' said Wellgunde. 'It's Siegfried. What a nerve!'

'Why shouldn't he be Siegfried if he wants to?' whispered Woglinde. 'I think it suits him.'

'Oh, well.' Flosshilde shrugged her slim shoulders. 'Here we go again.'

Malcolm was shaking Joe Ayres by the hand and saying 'Well done'. Joe Ayres winced as he withdrew his hand; he suspected that the German's ferocious grip had dislocated one of his knuckles.

'It could have been worse,' said Flosshilde, 'considering . . .' She stopped suddenly, and poked Wellgunde's arm. 'Look,' she hissed, 'over there, by the pear tree. Look who it is!'

'No!' Wellgunde's eyes were sparkling with excitement as she followed Flosshilde's pointing finger, and a pear on the tree ripened prematurely as a result. 'I don't believe it.'

'He doesn't look a day older,' said Woglinde, fondly.

The other two made faces at her.

Malcolm recognised Alberich at once. As the Prince of the Nibelungs approached him, Malcolm's heart seemed to collapse. Not that the Nibelung was a terrifying sight; a short, broad, grey-haired man in a dark overcoat, nothing more. There was no point in running away, and Malcolm stood his ground as Alberich approached and extended his hand for a handshake. Malcolm closed his fist around the Ring and put his hands behind his back.

'I'm sorry,' said Alberich in German. 'I thought you were someone else.'

'Oh, yes?'

'Someone I used to know in Germany, as a matter of fact. You look very like him, from a distance. But perhaps he was a little bit taller.'

'I don't think so,' said Malcolm without thinking.

Alberich laughed. 'How would you know? But you're right, actually. He wasn't.'

'My name is Manfred Finger,' Malcolm managed to say. 'I own the Hall.'

'Hans Albrecht.' Alberich smiled again. 'I'm afraid I don't know many people in England. But perhaps you know a friend of mine who lives near here.'

'I'm afraid I don't know many people either,' said Malcolm, forcing himself to smile. 'I've only been here a short while myself.'

'Well, this friend of mine is a very remarkable person, so perhaps you do know him. Malcolm Fisher. Familiar?'

'Any friend of Malcolm's is a friend of mine,' said Malcolm truthfully. 'But I don't remember him mentioning you.'

'That's so like him.' Alberich was massaging the fourth finger of his right hand as if it was hurting. 'Arthritis,' he explained. 'Anyway, if you see him before I do, you might remind him that he's got something of mine. A gold ring, and a hat. Both valueless, but I'd like them back.'

'I'm afraid Malcolm hasn't been quite himself lately,' said Malcolm. 'But I'll remind him if I see him before you do.'

'Would you? That's very kind. And do give him my best wishes.' Alberich turned to go, then stopped. 'Oh, and by the way,' he said in English. 'Well done. I liked your horse. Goodbye.'

As if that wasn't bad enough, Malcolm heard on the late news that two airliners had missed each other by inches over Manchester that afternoon. Had they collided, said the announcer, more than five hundred people would probably have lost their lives. An inquiry was being held, but the probable cause of the incident was human error.

6

Against the dark blue night sky above the Mendip Hills, someone with bright eyes might have been able to make out two tiny black dots, which could conceivably have been ravens, except of course that they were far too high up.

'It was around here somewhere,' said Thought.

'That's what you said last time,' said Memory. His pinions were aching, and he hadn't eaten for sixteen hours. During that time, he and his colleague had been round the world twenty-four times. Anything the sun could do, it seemed, they could do better.

'All right, then,' said Thought, 'don't believe me, see if I care. But he's down there somewhere, I know he is. I definitely heard the Ring calling.'

'That was probably Radio Bristol,' said Memory. Exhaustion had made him short-tempered.

They flew on in silence, completing a circuit of the counties of Somerset, Avon and Devon. Finally, they could go no further, and swooped down onto the roof of a thatched barn just outside Dulverton.

'How come you can hear the Ring, anyway?' said Memory. 'I can't.'

'Nor me, usually. It just sort of happens, once in a while. But it never lasts long enough for me to get an exact fix on it.'

A foolhardy bat fluttered towards them, curious to know who these strangers might be. The two ravens turned and stared at it, frightening it out of its wits.

'If it's about the radio licence,' said the bat, 'there's a cheque in the post.'

'Get lost,' said Memory, and the bat did its best to obey. Being gifted with natural radar, however, it did not find it easy.

'Wotan's in a terrible state these days,' said Thought. 'Not happy at all.'

'So what's new?'

'He's been all over the shop looking for clues. Went down a tin-mine in Bolivia the other day, came out all covered in dust.'

'I could have told him he'd do no good in Bolivia,' said Memory. 'Perhaps it would be better if we split up. That way we could cover more ground. You take one hemisphere, I take the other, sort of thing.'

Thought considered this for a moment. 'No, wouldn't work. You couldn't think where to go, and I couldn't remember where I'd been. Waste of everybody's time.'

'Please yourself.'

'You want to go off on your own then, or what?'

'Forget it.'

Thought was about to say something, but stopped. 'Listen,' he whispered. 'Did you hear that?'

'What?'

'It's the Ring again. Somewhere over there.' He pointed with his wing to the east. 'Not too far away, either.'

'How far?'

'Dunno, it's stopped again.'

Memory shook his head. 'I'm thinking of packing all this in,' he said.

'How do you mean?' said Thought.

'All this flying about, and that. I mean, where's it getting me?'

'It's a living, though.'

'Is it?' Memory leaned forward and snapped up a moth. It tasted sour. 'You take my brother-in-law. Talentless little git if you ask me. Used to run errands for the Moon-Goddess. Then they got one of those telexes, and he was out on his ear. So he set up this courier service – five years ago, give or take a bit – and look at him now. Nest in the tallest forest in Saxony, another in the Ardennes for the winter, and I bet he isn't eating moths.'

'Nests aren't everything,' said Thought. 'There's job satisfaction. There's travel. There's service to the community.'

'I know,' said Memory. 'Instead of all this fooling about, why don't we keep an eye on the girls, or Alberich? Maybe they know something we don't.'

Thought considered this. 'Could do,' he said, 'it's worth a try . . .' He stopped, and both birds were silent for a moment. 'There it goes again. Definitely over there somewhere.'

'Stuff it,' said Memory. 'Let's find the Rhinedaughters.'

Malcolm found it difficult to sleep that night. He had managed to get the thought of the two airliners out of his mind, but the meeting with Alberich was not so lightly dismissed. He had been afraid, more so than ever before, and the terrible thing was that he could not understand why. He was taller and stronger than the Nibelung, and he had the ability to make himself taller and stronger yet if the need arose. That was the whole point of the Tarnhelm. But the Nibelung had something else that made his own magic powers seem irrelevant; he had authority, and that was not something Malcolm could afford to ignore.

He looked at his watch; it was half-past two in the morning. He toyed with the idea of transporting himself to Los Angeles or Adelaide, where it would be light and he could get a cup of coffee without waking up the house-keeper. He was on the point of doing this when he heard a noise in the corridor outside.

Combe Hall was full of unexplained noises, which everyone he asked attributed to the plumbing. But something told Malcolm that plumbing made gurgling noises, not stealthy creeping noises. Without understanding why, he knew that he was in danger, and something told him that it was probably the right time for him to become invisible.

His bedroom door was locked, and he stood beside it. Outside, he could hear footsteps, which stopped. There was a scrabbling sound, a click and the door opened gently. He recognised the face of Alberich, peering into the room, and for a moment was rooted to the spot. Then it occurred to him that he was considerably bigger than Alberich, and also invisible. The Nibelung crept into the room and tiptoed over to the bed. As he bent over it, Malcolm kicked him hard.

It would be unfair to Malcolm to say that he did not know his own strength. He knew his own strength very well (or rather his lack of it) but as yet he had not come to terms with the strength of Siegfried the Dragon-Slayer. As a result, he hit Alberich very hard indeed. The intruder uttered a loud yelp and fell over.

Malcolm was horrified. His first reaction was that he must have killed Alberich, but a loud and uncomplicated complaint from his victim convinced him that that was not so. His next reaction was to apologise.

'Sorry,' he said. 'What the hell do you think you're doing?'

'You clumsy idiot,' said the Prince of the Nibelungs, 'you've broken my leg.'

It occurred to Malcolm that this served Alberich right, and he said so. In fact, he suggested, Alberich was extremely lucky to get off so lightly, since presumably he had broken in with the intention of committing murder.

'Don't be stupid,' said Alberich. 'I only wanted the Ring.'

He made it sound as if he had just dropped by to borrow a bowl of sugar. 'Now, about my broken leg . . .'

'Never mind your broken leg.'

'I mind it a lot. Get a doctor.'

'You're taking a lot for granted, aren't you?' said Malcolm sternly. 'You're my deadliest enemy. Why shouldn't I . . .

72

well, dispose of you, right now?'

Alberich laughed. 'You?' he said incredulously. 'Who do you think you are, Jack the Ripper?'

'I could be if I wanted to,' said Malcolm. The Nibelung ignored him.

'You wouldn't hurt a fly,' he sneered. 'That's your trouble. You'll never get anywhere in this world unless you improve your attitude. And did no-one ever tell you it's bad manners to be invisible when someone's talking to you?'

'You sound just like my mother,' said Malcolm.

He reappeared, and Alberich glowered at him. 'Still pretending to be who you aren't, I see,' he said.

'I'll be who I want to be. I'm not afraid of you any more.'

'Delighted to hear it. Perhaps you'll fetch a doctor now.'

'And the police,' said Malcolm, to frighten him. 'You're a burglar.'

'You wouldn't dare,' replied Alberich, but Malcolm could see he was worried. This was remarkable. A few minutes ago, he had been paralysed with fear. Now he found the whole thing vaguely comic. Still, it would be as well to call a doctor. He went to the telephone beside his bed.

'Not that sort of doctor,' said Alberich, irritably. 'What do you think I am, human?'

'So what sort of doctor do you want?' Malcolm asked.

'A proper doctor. A Nibelung.'

'Fine. And how do you suggest I set about finding one, look in the Yellow Pages?'

'Don't be facetious. Use the Ring.'

'Can I do that?' Malcolm was surprised by this.

'Of course you can. Just rub the Ring against your nose and call for a doctor.'

Feeling rather foolish, Malcolm did what he was told. At once, a short, stocky man with very pale skin materialised beside him, wearing what appeared to be a sack.

'You called?' said the Nibelung.

'Where did you come from?' Malcolm asked.

'Nibelheim, where do you think? So where's the patient?'

The doctor did something to Alberich's leg with a spanner and a jar of ointment, and disappeared as suddenly as he had come.

'That's handy,' Malcolm said. 'Can I just summon Nibelungs when I want to?'

'Of course,' said Alberich. 'Although why you should want to is another matter. By and large, they're incredibly boring people.'

Malcolm shrugged his shoulders. 'Anyway, how's your leg?' he asked.

'Very painful. But it's healed.'

'*Healed?* But I thought you said it was broken.'

'So it was,' replied Alberich, calmly. 'And now it's unbroken again. That's what the doctor was for. It'll be stiff for a day or so, of course, but that can't be helped. If you will go around kicking people, you must expect to cause anguish and suffering.'

Malcolm yawned. 'In that case, you can go away and leave me in peace,' he said. 'And don't let me catch you around here again, or there'll be trouble.'

This bravado didn't convince anyone. Alberich made no attempt to move, but sat on the floor rubbing his knee, until Malcolm, unable to think of anything else to do, offered him a drink.

'I thought you'd never ask,' said Alberich. 'I'll have a large schnapps, neat.'

'I don't think I've got any of that,' said Malcolm.

'You're supposed to be a German. Oh well, whatever comes to hand, so long as it isn't sherry. I don't like sherry.'

So it was that Malcolm found himself sharing a bottle of gin with the Prince of Nibelheim at three o'clock in the morning. It was not something he would have chosen to do, especially after a tiring day, but the mere fact that he was able to do it was remarkable enough. Alberich made no further attempt to relieve him of the Ring; he didn't even mention the subject until Malcolm himself raised it. Instead, he talked mostly about his health, or to be precise, his digestion.

'Lobster,' he remarked more than once, 'gives me the most appalling heartburn. And gooseberries . . .'

In short, there was nothing to fear from Alberich, and Malcolm found himself feeling rather sorry for the Nibelung, who, by his own account at least, had had rather a hard time.

'It wasn't the gold I wanted,' he said. 'I wanted to get my own back on those damned women.'

'Which women?'

'The Rhinedaughters. I won't bore you with all the details. Not a nice story.' Alberich helped himself to some more gin. 'There I was, taking a stroll beside the Rhine on a pleasant summer evening, and these three girls, with no more clothes on than would keep a fly warm . . .'

'I know all that,' said Malcolm.

'Do you?' said Alberich, rather disappointed. 'Oh well, never mind. But it wasn't the power or the money I wanted – well, they would have been nice, I grant you, I'm not saying they wouldn't – but it's the principle of the thing. You know how it is when someone takes something away from you without any right to it at all. You feel angry. You feel hard done by. And if that thing is the control of the world, you feel very hard done by indeed. Not that I *want* to control the world particularly – I imagine I'd do it very badly. But it's like not being invited to a party, you feel hard done by even if you wouldn't have gone if they'd asked you. I know I'm not explaining this very well . . . You can get obsessive about it, you know? Especially if you've thought about nothing else for the last thousand years.'

'Couldn't you have done something else, to take your mind off it? Got a job, or something?'

'This may seem strange, but having been master of the world for forty-eight hours – that's how long they let me keep the Ring, you know – doesn't really qualify you for much. And they threw me out of Nibelheim.'

'Did they?'

'They did. You can't really blame them. I had enslaved them and made them mine gold for me. They weren't best pleased.'

'So what have you been doing ever since?'

'Moping about, mostly, feeling sorry for myself. And looking for the Ring, of course. And a bit of freelance metallurgy, just to keep the wolf from the door. My card.'

He took a card from his wallet. 'Hans Albrecht and partners,' it read, 'Mining Engineers and Contractors, Est. AD 900.'

'Most people think the date's a misprint,' said Alberich, 'but it's not. Anyway, that's what I've been doing, and a thoroughly wretched time I've had, too.'

'Have another drink,' Malcolm suggested.

'You're too kind,' said Alberich. 'Mind you, if I have too much to drink these days, it plays hell with my digestion. Did I tell you about that?'

'Yes.'

Alberich shook his head sadly. 'I'm boring you, I can tell. But let me tell you something useful. Even if you won't give me the Ring, don't let Wotan get his hands on it.'

'I wasn't planning to,' said Malcolm. 'Another?'

'Why not? And then I must be going. It's late, and you've been a horse all afternoon. That's tiring, I know. Now, about Wotan. I don't know how you've managed it, but you've got the Ring to do what you want it to. Not what I had intended when I made it, let me say. In fact, I can't remember what I intended when I made it. It's been a long time. Anyway. Is there any tonic left?'

'No. Sorry.'

'Doesn't matter. About Wotan. He's devious, very devious, but if you've got the Ring on your side . . .'

Malcolm thought of something incredibly funny. 'I haven't got the Ring on my *side*,' he said, 'I've got it on my *finger*.'

They had a good laugh over that. 'No, but seriously,' said

Alberich, 'if you can make the Ring do what you want it to, then there's nothing Wotan can do to you unless you want him to.'

'But I don't want him to do anything to me. I want him to go away.'

'That's what you think. Like I said, Wotan's devious. Devious devious *devious*. He'll get you exactly where he wants you unless you're very careful, I assure you.'

'How?'

'That, my friend, remains to be seen. The days of armed force and violence are long gone, I'm sorry to say. It's cleverness that gets results. It's the same in the mining industry. Did I tell you about that?'

'Yes,' Malcolm lied. 'Go on about Wotan.'

Alberich looked at the bottom of his glass. Unfortunately, there was nothing to obscure his view of it. He picked up the bottle, but it was empty.

'I am going to have raging indigestion all tomorrow,' he said sadly. 'Don't let them tell you there's no such thing as spontaneous combustion. I suffer from it continually. Wotan can't take the Ring from you, but he can make you give it to him of your own free will. And before you ask me, I don't know how he'll do it, but he'll think of something. Have you got any Bisodol?'

'I can get you a sandwich.'

'A sandwich? Do you want to kill me as well as breaking my leg? No, don't you let go of the Ring, Malcolm Fisher. If I can't have it, you might as well keep it. It'll be safe with you until you're ready to give it to me.'

Malcolm looked uncomfortable at this. Alberich laughed.

'Of your own free will, I mean. But that won't happen until it isn't a symbol of power any more, only a bit of old jewellery. It'll happen, though, you mark my words. See how it ends.'

'How do you know?'

'I don't.' Alberich rose unsteadily to his feet. 'Time I was going.'

'How's your leg?'

'My leg? Oh, that's fine, it's my stomach I'm worried about. I'm always worried about my stomach. We sulphur-dwarves were created out of the primal flux of the earth's core. We have always existed, and we will always exist, in some form or other. You can kill us, of course, but unless you do, we live for ever. The problem is, if you're made largely of sulphur, you are going to suffer from heartburn, and there's nothing at all you can do about it. Over the past however many it is million years, I have tried absolutely every remedy for dyspepsia that has ever been devised, and they're all useless. All of them. In all the years I've been alive, there was only one time I didn't have indigestion. You know when that was? The forty-eight hours when I had the Ring. Good night.'

'You can stay here if you like,' said Malcolm.

'That's kind of you, but I've got a room over at the Blue Boar. The fresh air will clear my head. I'll see myself out.'

'That reminds me. How did you get in here?'

'Through the front door. I have a way with locks.'

'And how did you find me in the first place?'

'Easy. I smelt the Ring. Once you started using it, that was no problem.'

Alberich went to the door, then turned. 'Do you know something, Malcolm Fisher?' he said. 'It goes against the grain saying this, but I like you. In a way. Up to a point. You can keep the Ring for the time being. I like what you're doing with it.'

Malcolm wanted to say something but could think of nothing.

'And if ever there's anything . . . Oh, forget it. Good luck.'

A few minutes later, Malcolm heard the front door slam. He got back into bed and switched off the light. It was nearly morning, and he was very tired.

Two ravens were perched on the telegraph pole outside the Blue Boar in Combe.

'It's definitely coming from near here somewhere,' said Thought.

Memory had been listening for the Voice all day, and he no longer believed in it. 'You've been overdoing it,' he said. 'Maybe you should take a couple of days off. We can't hear the Ring, either of us. It's not possible.'

In the road below, a short, heavily-built man was waiting for the night porter to open the door of the hotel. Thought flapped his wings to attract his partner's attention.

'Look,' he whispered, 'down there.'

'It's Alberich,' replied Memory. 'What's he doing here?'

'I told you,' said Thought. 'I told you and you wouldn't . . .'

'All right, all right,' said Memory uneasily. 'Doesn't prove anything, does it? I mean, he could be here for some totally different reason.'

'Such as?'

Memory stared blankly at his claws. 'Dunno,' he said. 'But it still doesn't mean . . .'

'Come on,' said Thought, 'we've found him. He's somewhere in this village. We'd better tell Wotan.'

'Oh no.' Memory shook his head. 'You can if you like. If we're wrong, and Wotan comes flogging out here on a fool's errand . . .'

'So what do we do?'

They racked their brains for a moment, but in vain. Then Thought had a sudden inspiration. 'I know,' he said. 'We'll tell Loge. Then it'll be his duty to pass the message on to the Boss.'

The two ravens laughed, maliciously.

7

Alberich woke up next morning with a thick head, a weary heart, and indigestion. He took a taxi to Taunton, only to find that he had missed the London train, and was faced with an hour in one of the dreariest towns he had ever come across in the course of a very long life.

The only possible solution was a cup or two of strong, drinkable coffee, and he set off to find it. As he sat in a grimly coy coffee shop in Kingston Road, he tried to turn over in his mind the various courses of action still open to him, but found that rational thought was not possible in his state of health and the centre of Taunton. He gave it up, and as he did so became aware of a familiar voice behind him:

'Really,' it was saying, 'nobody's worn that shade of blue since the twelfth century. I *couldn't* go out looking like that.'

'You should have thought of that earlier,' said another voice, just as familiar. 'You're impossible sometimes.'

The last time Alberich had heard those two voices, and the third voice that broke in to contradict them both, was in the depths of the Rhine, about a thousand years ago. He turned round slowly.

'What are you three doing here?' he asked.

Flosshilde smiled sweetly at him, with the result that the milk in his coffee turned to cream. 'Hello, Alberich,' she said. 'How's the digestion?'

'Awful. What are you doing here?'

'Drinking coffee. What about you?'

'Don't be flippant.'

80

'But that's what we do best,' said Woglinde, also smiling. There was little point to this, except pure malice, for Alberich had forsworn Love and was therefore immune to all smiles, even those of Rhinedaughters. But Woglinde smiled anyway, as a sportsman who can find no pheasants will sometimes take a shot at a passing crow. 'We're too set in our ways to change now.'

'What are you doing here?' Alberich asked.

'That would be telling,' said Wellgunde, twitching her nose like a rabbit. 'How about you?'

'Tourism,' said Alberich with a shudder. 'I like grim, miserable places where there's nothing at all to do.'

'You would,' said Flosshilde. That, so far as she was concerned, closed the subject. But Wellgunde was rather more cautious.

'We're out shopping,' she said artlessly. 'Everyone's looking to Taunton for colours this season.'

'In fact,' said Flosshilde, 'Taunton is the place where it's all happening these days.' She giggled, and Wellgunde kicked her under the table.

Alberich shook his head, which was a rash move on his part. 'You'll find it harder than you imagine,' he said. 'You won't be able to trap him easily.'

'Trap who?'

Alberich ignored her. 'What you fail to take into account,' he continued, 'is his extreme lack of self-confidence. Even if he does fall in love with one or all of you, he's highly unlikely to feel up to doing anything about it. He'll just go home and feel miserable. And then what will you have achieved?'

'We're not like that,' said Woglinde. 'We're good at dealing with shy people.'

Alberich laughed and rose to his feet. 'I wish you luck,' he said.

'No, you don't,' said Wellgunde shrewdly.

'Let me rephrase that. You'll need luck. Lots of it. See you in another thousand years.'

'Not if we see you first,' said Flosshilde cheerfully. 'Have a nice day.'

One of the few luxuries that Malcolm had indulged in since his acquisition of limitless wealth was a brand new sports car. He had always wanted one, although now that he had it he found that he was rather unwilling to go above thirty miles an hour in it. The whole point of having a car, however, as any psychologist will tell you, is that it represents Defended Space, where no-one can get at you, and Malcolm always felt happier once he was behind the wheel. There were risks, of course; driving in Somerset, that county of narrow lanes and leisurely tractors, can cause impatience and bad temper, which Malcolm was in duty bound to avoid.

Once his headache had subsided, Malcolm thought it would make a change to go into Taunton and look at the shops. He had been an enthusiastic window-shopper all his life, and now that he could afford to buy not only the things in the shop-windows but the shops themselves if he wanted to, he enjoyed this activity even more. Not that he ever did buy anything, of course; the habits of a lifetime are not so easily broken.

For example, he stood for quite five minutes outside the fishing-tackle shop in Silver Street looking at all the elegant and attractive paraphernalia in the window. At least two rivers, possibly three, ran through the grounds of the Hall, and fishing was supposed to be a relaxing occupation which soothed the nerves and the temper. Not that he particularly wanted to catch or persecute fish; but it would at least be an interest, with things to learn and things to buy. For the same reason, he had a good look at the camera shop in St James Street, and he only stopped himself from going inside by reflecting that he had nobody to take pictures of, except perhaps the English Rose.

He walked by the auction-rooms, and wondered who

was doing his old job now. Inside there would be Liz, cataloguing something or other, and Philip Wilcox, training, not very energetically, to be an auctioneer. Again, he felt a strong temptation to go inside and look at them, and that would be perfectly reasonable, since they both knew him only as the rich German who had bought the Hall. He could now afford to buy everything in the sale if he wanted to. But the sale today was of antique clocks, and he already knew only too well how slowly the time passed. Besides, there was no point in buying anything for himself (it was, after all, Only Him) and he had no-one else to buy things for.

As he walked down North Street towards what passes for a centre, he noticed a shop that he could not recall having seen before. It was one of those art and craft places, selling authentic pottery and ethnic clothes (hence no doubt its name, Earth 'n' Wear). But shops of that kind are always springing up and disappearing like mayflies in upwardly-mobile towns, and Taunton is nothing if not upwardly-mobile. In fact, as they will be delighted to tell you, Taunton is no longer a one-horse town; these days, they have a bicycle as well . . .

Entirely out of curiosity, since he was safe in the knowledge that there would not be anything in a shop of this sort that he could conceivably want to buy, Malcolm opened the door, which had goat-bells behind it, and went in. The place was empty, except for a ghostly string quartet playing Mozart, a large cat asleep on a pile of Indian cotton shirts, and an astoundingly pretty girl with red hair sitting behind the till. As soon as Malcolm walked through the door, she looked up from the poem she was writing in a spiral-bound notebook with a stylised cat on the cover and smiled at him.

Malcolm had always been of the opinion that pretty girls should not be allowed to smile at people unless they meant something by it, for it gives them an unfair advantage. He now felt under an obligation to buy something. That

83

presumably was why the owner had installed a pretty girl in the shop in the first place, and Malcolm did not approve. It was exploitation of the worst sort.

'Feel free to look around,' said the girl.

Malcolm walked briskly to the back of the shop and tried to appear profoundly interested in beeswax candles. Although he had his back to her, he felt sure that the girl was still looking at him, and he remembered that he was the most handsome man in the world, which might account for it. A smirk tried to get onto his face, but he sent it away. He was, he assured himself, only imagining it, and even if he wasn't, there was bound to be a catch in it all somewhere. This was Taunton, not Hollywood.

For her part, Wellgunde was rather dismayed. Either her smile had gone wrong since she checked it that morning, or else this young man was immune to smiles, which would be a pity. She had gone to the trouble of materialising this shop and all its contents just in order to be able to have somewhere to smile at the Ring-Bearer. A shop, the Rhinedaughters had decided, made an ideal trap for ensnaring unwary Ring-Bearers. Perhaps they had under-estimated him, Wellgunde thought. Certainly it had seemed a very straightforward project when they discussed it that morning. From all they had learnt about him, Ingolf's Bane was a foolish, sentimental and susceptible young man who would as instinctively fall in love with a pretty girl who smiled at him as a trout snaps at a fly. The only point at issue in their planning session had been which one of them should have the dubious privilege of being the fly. They had tried drawing lots, but Woglinde would insist on cheating. They had tried tossing for it, but Flosshilde had winked at the coin, and it kept coming down in her favour. So finally they had decided to make a game of it: whoever captivated the Ring-Bearer first would have to see the job through, but the others would buy her lunch at Maxim's.

To make it a fair contest, they had materialised three

shops in the centre of Taunton. It was a reasonable bet that no-one would notice three shops suddenly appearing out of nowhere in the centre of town, for Taunton is like that, and it would be up to the Ring-Bearer to decide which one he went into first, and so who should have the first go.

Wellgunde frowned. She was going to have to make an effort.

'Are you looking for anything in particular?' she said sweetly.

There was another potential customer outside, looking through the window at a selection of herbal teas. She turned quickly and smiled at the door. The card obligingly flipped round to read 'Closed'. Things generally did what she wanted them to when she smiled at them.

'A present for my mother,' Malcolm replied, amazing himself with his own inventiveness.

'Does she like cats?' Wellgunde suggested. 'Most mothers do.'

'Yes, she does.'

'Then how about a spaghetti-jar with a cat on the front, or a tea-cosy in the shape of a cat, or a little china cat you can keep paperclips in, or a cat-shaped candle, or a Cotswold cat breadboard? We haven't got any framed cat woodcuts at the moment, but we're expecting a delivery this afternoon if you're not in a hurry.'

'That's a lot of cats,' said Malcolm startled.

'Cats and Cotswolds,' said the Rhinedaughter, brightly. 'You can sell anything with a cat or a Cotswold on it, although some people prefer rabbits.'

She smiled again, so brightly that Malcolm could feel the skin on his face turning brown. He began to feel distinctly uncomfortable.

'I'd better have one of those oven-gloves,' he mumbled.

'With a cat on it?'

'Yes, please.'

The girl seemed rather hurt as she took Malcolm's money, and he wondered what he had said.

85

'If she doesn't like it, I can change it for you,' said the girl. 'No trouble, really.'

'I'm sure she'll like it. She's very fond of cats. And cooking.'

'Goodbye, then.'

'Goodbye.'

Wellgunde watched him go, and frowned. 'Oh well,' she said to herself, 'bother him, then.'

She smiled at the shop, and just to please her it vanished into thin air. Then she walked down to the banks of the Tone and dived gracefully into its khaki waters.

'Well,' said one old lady to another as a chain of silver bubbles rose to the surface, 'you don't see so much of that sort of thing nowadays.'

Confused, Malcolm turned up Hammet Street. It was not surprising, he said to himself, that a girl, even a pretty one, should want to smile at someone looking exactly like Siegfried the Dragon-Slayer. And it was Siegfried's appearance, not his, that she had been smiling at, so really the smile was nothing to do with him. Besides, it was probably just a smile designed to sell cat-icons, in which it had succeeded admirably. He felt in his pocket for the oven-glove, but it didn't seem to be there any more. He must have dropped it. What a pity, never mind.

At the junction of Hammet Street and Magdalene Street, there was a health-food shop which had not been there yesterday. Of that Malcolm was absolutely certain, because he had parked his car beside the kerb on which the shop was now standing. He stood very still and frowned.

'Did I do that?' he said aloud. 'And if so, how?'

He knew the song about the girl who left trees and flowers lying about wherever she had gone; but trees and flowers are one thing, health-food shops are another. Either it had been built very, very quickly (after his recent experiences with builders at the Hall, Malcolm doubted this) or else it had appeared out of nowhere, or else he was hallucinating. He crossed the road and went in.

'Hello there,' said the bewilderingly pretty girl behind the counter. 'Can I help you?'

It was probably the dazzling smile that made Malcolm realise what was going on. 'Hang on a moment, please,' he said, and walked out again. Next door was a furniture shop with a big plate-glass window. Fortunately, the street was deserted, and Malcolm was able to turn himself into the three Rhinedaughters without being observed. He found that he recognised two of them immediately. As an experiment, he smiled a Rhinedaughter smile at a chest of drawers in the shop window. It seemed to glow for a moment, and then its polyurethane finish was changed into a deep French polish shine.

'That explains it,' he said to himself, and did not allow himself to think that although that explained the smiles he had been getting, it did not explain the shops that had appeared from nowhere. Take care of the smiles, after all, and the shops will take care of themselves. He understood that the Rhinedaughters, the original owners of the gold from which the Ring was made, were after him, and their smiles were baits to draw him to his doom. Not that there weren't worse dooms, he reflected, but he had the world to consider.

Instead of walking away, however, he turned and went back into the health-food shop. Now that he knew that the smiles were only another aspect of this rather horrible game that Life was playing with him, and not genuine expressions of interest by pretty girls, he felt that he could deal with the situation, for he had a supreme advantage over the previous owners of the Nibelung's Ring. He had no vanity, no high opinion of himself which these creatures could use as the basis for their attack. All that remained was for him to deal with them before they did anything more troublesome than smiling.

'Hello again,' said Woglinde.

'Which one are you, then?' he replied, smiling back. Woglinde looked at him for a moment, and then burst into tears, burying her face in her small pink hands. Instinctively, Malcolm was horrified; then he remembered Hagen, Alberich's son, whom the three Rhinedaughters had drowned in the flood, singing sweetly all the while.

'Thought so,' he said, trying to sound unpleasant (but he had lost the knack). 'So which one are you?'

'Woglinde,' sobbed the girl. 'And now you're all cross.'

The Rhinedaughter sniffed, looked up angrily, and smiled like a searchlight. A carnation appeared in Malcolm's buttonhole, but his resolve was unaffected.

'You can cut that out,' he said.

'Oh, well,' said Woglinde, and Malcolm could see no tears in her deep blue eyes. He could see many other things, but no tears, and the other things were rather hazardous, so he ignored them.

'Where did the shop come from?' he asked.

'Shan't tell you,' said Woglinde, coyly frowning. 'You're beastly and I hate you.'

'Girls don't talk like that any more,' said Malcolm. 'A thousand years ago perhaps, but not in the nineteen-eighties.'

'This girl does,' replied Woglinde. 'It's part of her charm. You've been looking for a nice old-fashioned girl all your life and now you've found one.'

Put like that, the proposition (accompanied by the brightest smile yet) was somewhat startling, and Malcolm turned away and looked at a display of organic pulses.

'You've been to a lot of trouble,' he said.

'I spent ages making it all nice for you,' said Woglinde.

'I don't like health food. Especially organic rice.'

'Oh, I'm *sorry*,' said Woglinde, petulantly. 'If I'd known, I'd have built you a chip-shop instead.' She checked herself; she was letting her temper interfere with business. 'I still can, if you'd rather.'

'I wouldn't bother, if I were you,' said Malcolm. 'I expect you're sick of the sight of fish.'

'If you asked me to I would.'

'Forget it, please. I know what you want, and you can't have it.'

'Usually that's our line,' said the Rhinedaughter casually. Malcolm blushed. 'Oh go on,' she continued, 'it's our Ring, really.'

Perhaps the smiles had a cumulative effect. Malcolm suddenly felt a terrible urge to give her the Ring. He had already taken it off his finger before he knew what he was doing, and it was only when he caught sight of her face, like a kitten watching a beetle it intends to eat, that he felt the sense of danger. He thrust the Ring back on, so fiercely that he cut the skin between his fingers.

'I can't,' he said, sadly. 'I'd love to, but I can't. You wouldn't want it, really.'

Woglinde suddenly laughed, and Malcolm felt as if he was being smothered in gossamer, like a fly trapped by a spider. 'Don't be silly,' she cooed, 'I'd like it more than anything in the whole wide world. I think you're *mean*.'

Again there was a hideous temptation to give in, so strong that the Ring seemed to burn his skin. Malcolm could stand it no longer, and tried to command the Tarnhelm to take him away. But his mind could not issue the order; the smiles had got into it, as light gets into photographic film, and blurred all the edges. 'Stop that!' he shouted, and Woglinde winced as if he had slapped her. He tightened his hand round the Ring, and her face seemed to collapse. Suddenly, she was not pretty at all; she looked like a thousand-year-old teenager who wanted something she knew she couldn't have. Then, just as suddenly, she was lovelier than ever, and Malcolm knew that she had given up.

'Sorry,' he said, 'but there it is.'

He turned and walked out of the shop, trying not to look back, but the urge was too strong. When he did look back, however, the shop was gone. He had won this bout, then; but was that all? It would probably be unwise to go swimming for a week or so . . .

After the fight, Malcolm needed a drink. He walked swiftly up Canon Street, heading for his favourite pub. But it wasn't there any more; instead, there was one of those very chic little wine-bars that come like shadows and so depart all over England. He had a horrible idea that he knew where this one had come from.

The wine-bar ('Le Cochonnet') was empty except for a quite unutterably pretty girl behind the bar, tenderly polishing a glass.

'You can put it all back exactly as it was,' said Malcolm, sternly.

The girl stared at him in amazement, and for a moment Malcolm wondered if he had made a mistake. But he looked at the girl again, and recognised the third Rhinedaughter. There couldn't be two girls like that in the world, unless he was very lucky.

'So which are you,' he said, 'Wellgunde or Flosshilde?'

'Flosshilde,' said the girl, carelessly. 'You've met the other two?'

'That's right.' He held up his right hand, letting the light play on the ring, 'And I'm not going to give it to you, either. It's not a toy, you know.'

Flosshilde studied the glass in her hand for a moment. 'All right,' she said. 'If you insist. Would you like a drink?'

Flosshilde had been rather proud of her wine-bar, and it was with great reluctance that she had agreed to change it back into the French Horn. But she did so with a smile.

'Won't the landlord and the customers be a bit disorientated?' Malcolm asked.

'Not really,' said Flosshilde. 'All I did was change them into chairs and tables, and they won't have felt anything. For some reason, when I smile at people and change them, they don't seem to mind.'

'I can understand that,' said Malcolm. 'Let me buy you a drink.'

'I'll have a Babycham,' said Flosshilde. 'No ice.'

When he returned with the drinks, Flosshilde leaned forward and whispered, 'Your Liz is over there in the corner with her boyfriend. The one you threw in the water.'

'So what?' said Malcolm coldly. 'She's not my Liz.'

'I could turn him into a frog for you, if you like,' whispered Flosshilde. 'Or I could smile at him without turning him into a frog. Your Liz wouldn't like that at all.'

'I'd rather you didn't,' said Malcolm. 'I'm not allowed to be malicious any more.'

'That sounds awful.' Flosshilde seemed genuinely sorry for him. 'Would it count if I did it?'

'Probably. But it's kind of you to offer.'

'Any time. I might just do it anyway. I don't like him, he's stuffy. I don't like stuffy people.'

'I'd better be careful, then,' said Malcolm. 'I've become very stuffy since . . .'

'That's not your fault,' said the Rhinedaughter.

'I shouldn't be doing this,' said Malcolm. 'Fraternising with the enemy.'

'I'm not really the enemy, am I?' Flosshilde smiled, but it wasn't a serious smile, just a movement of the lips intended to convey friendliness. Malcolm was intrigued.

'I mean, you're not going to give me the Ring, and why should you? That doesn't mean I hate you.'

'Doesn't it?'

'Course not.'

'Woglinde burst out crying.'

'She does that,' said Flosshilde. 'She's very bad-tempered. I'll tell her to leave you alone.'

'Would you?' Malcolm felt a strange sensation at the back of his head, a sort of numbness. He hadn't chatted like this to anyone for a long time.

'Are you staying in England long?' he asked, trying to sound uninterested.

Flosshilde grinned. 'If you like. It's the same for us, you know. We're all in the same boat. Of course, I've got the other two for company, but you know what it's like with sisters. They get on your nerves.'

'I know, I've got a sister.'

'Then we'll be company for each other,' Flosshilde said. 'I mean, we can go for drives in the country, or maybe take a boat up the river.'

Malcolm remembered Hagen, and said he didn't like boats. 'Won't your sisters mind?' he added nervously.

'Oh bother them,' said Flosshilde. 'Besides, I can tell them I'm working on you.'

'Will you be?'

'You'll have to wait and see,' said Flosshilde, carefully not smiling. 'Now, why don't you buy me lunch? I'm starving.'

Malcolm drove back to Combe Hall in a rather bewildered frame of mind, and nearly rammed a flock of sheep outside Bagborough. Over lunch, Flosshilde hadn't mentioned the Ring once, except in passing (she knew some very funny stories about the Gods, especially Wotan) and seemed to be making no effort at all to lead him to his doom. That, of course, might simply mean that she was being subtle; but Malcolm had taken the precaution of reading her thoughts, and although he knew that one shouldn't believe everything you read in people's minds, he had been rather taken aback by what he had found. Of course, it was possible that she had deliberately planted those thoughts there for him to read, but somehow he didn't think so.

It seemed that Flosshilde had reconciled herself to the fact that the Ring wasn't going to be given to her, and she didn't really mind. Instead, she rather liked the Ring-Bearer. Nothing more than that, but never mind. Nor was it simply his assumed shape that she liked; she had seen that

shape before when it had had the original Siegfried inside
it, and besides, she didn't judge by appearances. That, it
seemed, was not the way these curious other-worldly types
went about things, for in the world they inhabited, so many
people could change shape as easily as human beings
changed clothes, and so you could never be sure whether a
person was really handsome or simply smartly dressed.
Flosshilde, however, thought that she and the Ring-Bearer
might have something in common, and she wanted
someone nice to talk to and go out with. There had been
more than this, but Malcolm hadn't read it. He was saving it
up, to read over lunch tomorrow . . .

'Well?' said Woglinde. 'And where have you been?'

'Having lunch,' said Flosshilde, 'at Carey's.'

'But you haven't got it?' said Wellgunde abruptly.

'True.' Flosshilde lay back on the bed of the Tone and
blew bubbles. 'But who cares?'

Wellgunde stared at her sister, who closed her eyes and
let out a rather exaggerated sigh. 'I think I'm in love,' said
Flosshilde.

'Don't be ridiculous,' snapped Wellgunde. 'You can't be.
You aren't allowed to be.'

'Oh, all right then, I'm not. But the next best thing. Or the
next best thing to that. He's nice, in a quiet sort of way.'

'You should be ashamed of yourself,' said Woglinde,
fiercely; but Wellgunde smiled, confusing a shoal of min-
nows who happened to get in the way. 'If it makes it easier
for you to get the Ring,' she said softly, 'then you go ahead.'

'I'm not interested in the silly old Ring,' yawned Flosshilde. 'It's supremely unimportant.'

Wellgunde nodded. 'Of course. But it *would* be nicer to
have it than not to have it, now wouldn't it?'

'I suppose so.'

'And there's no point in your liking him if he doesn't like
you.'

Flosshilde made a vague grab at a passing roach, which

scuttled away. 'I don't know. Is there?'

'And if he likes you, he'll be pleased to give you the Ring, now won't he?'

'I don't know and I don't care,' replied Flosshilde. 'We're just good friends.'

'You've only met him once,' said Woglinde. 'There's no need to get soppy.'

'There's every need to get soppy. I like being soppy. What's for dinner?'

'Trout with almonds,' said Wellgunde.

'Not fish *again*.'

Wellgunde perched on the edge of a broken wardrobe, one of many that furnished the riverbed. 'Nobody says you shouldn't make friends,' she said gently. 'But what about us? We want our Ring back.'

'Once you've got it back, you can be friends with who you like,' said Woglinde, inspecting her toenails, 'though personally . . . They need doing again,' she added. 'There's something nasty in this river that dissolves coral pink.'

'Oh, be quiet, both of you,' said Flosshilde angrily. 'I'm sorry I told you now.'

There was silence at the bottom of the Tone for a while, with both Flosshilde and Woglinde sulking. Finally, Woglinde requested Wellgunde to ask her sister Flosshilde if she could borrow her coral pink nail varnish, and Flosshilde asked Wellgunde to tell her sister Woglinde that she couldn't.

'Be like that,' said Woglinde. 'See if I care.'

Flosshilde jumped up and floated to the surface.

'Now look what you've done,' hissed Wellgunde. 'You've offended her.'

'She isn't really in love, is she?' asked Woglinde nervously. 'That would be terrible.'

'I don't think so. She's just in one of her moods.'

'What'll we do?'

'Don't worry,' said Wellgunde calmly. 'Leave her to me.'

94

8

'Oh, for crying out loud,' said Wotan, putting down his fork with a bang, 'what do you want now?'

'Sorry,' panted Loge, breathless and sopping wet. 'I didn't realise you were still having breakfast.'

Wotan smiled wanly. 'Raining outside, is it?'

'Yes,' said Loge. 'Very heavily.'

'So what was so important it couldn't wait?'

'I think I'm on to something,' said Loge, sinking into a chair. The dining-room of Valhalla, the castle built by Fasolt and Fafner for the King of the Gods, was furnished in spartan but functional style. It had that air of grim and relentless spotlessness that is described as a woman's touch.

The Lord of Tempests looked at him suspiciously. 'If this turns out to be another wild goose chase,' he said, 'I'll turn you into a reservoir and stock you with rainbow trout.'

Loge shuddered. 'I'm sure there's something in this,' he managed to say. 'The ravens have sighted Alberich, and . . .'

'Aren't you going to offer your guest a cup of coffee?' Schwertleite the Valkyrie had come in with a crumb-brush and was ostentatiously brushing the table. 'I do wish you wouldn't bring work home with you.'

Wotan turned and glowered at his daughter, who took no notice. 'And ask him not to put his briefcase on the table.'

The Valkyrie swept out, and Wotan turned the full force of his glare on Loge. 'Now look what you've done,' he said. 'You've started her off.'

'But the ravens have seen Alberich and the Rhinedaughters, and they're in this village in England called . . .'

Schwertleite came back into the room with a bundle of newspapers in her arms. 'Ask your friend to sit on these,' she said sharply. 'I've just had those covers cleaned, although why I bother, I don't know.'

'Now you see what I have to put up with,' whispered Wotan. 'What's this about Alberich and the Rhinedaughters?'

Loge, perched uncomfortably on a pile of back numbers of *Die Zeit*, started to explain, but before he could get very far, the Valkyrie Grimgerde stalked into the room with a pot of coffee. She had resented making it, and it would just be left to get cold, but she had made it all the same. 'I'm doing you some scrambled eggs,' she said accusingly to Loge.

'Please, don't bother.'

'I've started now,' replied Grimgerde impatiently.

Loge was about to say thank you, but the Valkyrie had gone back into the kitchen. Almost at once, Schwertleite reappeared, with her arms folded.

'There are footmarks all over the kitchen floor,' she said icily. 'Have you been tracking in and out?'

Before Wotan could reply, she too had gone. Wotan's daughters had a habit of asking leading questions and disappearing before anyone could answer them. They had been doing it for over a thousand years, but it was still profoundly irritating.

'. . . in a little village called Combe,' said Loge, 'which is in Somerset. Now why else . . .?'

'What did you say?' Wotan hadn't been listening.

Loge took a deep breath, but could get no further. The Valkyrie Waltraute had come in with a plate of scrambled eggs. 'As if I didn't have enough to do,' she said, slamming the plate down. 'And mind the tablecloth.'

'Sorry,' said Loge.

'I wouldn't eat that if I were you,' Wotan muttered when

she had gone. 'None of my daughters can cook, although God knows it doesn't stop them. I can cook but I'm not allowed in the kitchen.'

Desperately, Loge wondered what to do so as to offend neither the Thunderer nor his daughters. He picked some scrambled egg up on his fork, but did not put it in his mouth.

'I've been putting up with this for eleven centuries,' continued Wotan. 'Much more of it and I shall go quite mad.'

'The ravens,' said Loge for the fourth time, 'have found Alberich and the Rhinedaughters, hanging around in a little village in . . .'

'It all started when their mother left me,' continued Wotan, 'and was I glad to see the back of her. But my dear daughters, all nine of them, decided that I needed looking after. They didn't want to, of course. They all wanted to have careers and lives of their own. I wanted them to have careers and lives of their own, preferably in another hemisphere.'

As if to prove his point, the Valkyrie Waltraute came storming in. 'You've been eating the bread again, haven't you?' she said bitterly.

'That's what it's there for.'

'You've started a new loaf when there was half a loaf left in the breadbin. Now I suppose I'll have to throw it out for the ravens.'

'Half a loaf is better than no bread,' Wotan roared after her as she stalked out again. A futile gesture. The Father of Battles banged his fist on the table, upsetting a coffee cup. A deep brown patch appeared on the tablecloth and Wotan turned white.

'You did that,' he said to Loge. 'If they ask, you did that. I've got to live in this house.'

Loge, whose titles include the Father of Lies, was not too keen on this particular falsehood, but the alternative was probably metamorphosis into a disused canal. He nodded meekly.

'So we've all been stuck in this wretched great barn of a place, miles from anywhere, driving each other mad for a thousand years,' said the King of the Gods. 'They hate it as much as I do, but they'll never move.'

'At least there are only eight of them now,' said Loge. 'It must have been far worse when Brunnhilde was . . .'

Loge fell silent, terrified lest his lack of tact should arouse Wotan's anger. But Wotan only laughed. 'You must be joking,' he said. 'Imagine my delight when I'd finally managed to get one of them off my hands – and no question, Brunnhilde was the worst – and I thought that perhaps they'd all go away and at last I'd be allowed to wear my comfortable shoes in the dining-room. I fixed that miserable child up with Siegfried the Dragon-Slayer, the most marvellous man who ever lived. And look what she did to him.'

Loge nodded sympathetically; tact was all that stood between him and a future in fish-farming.

'Mind you,' said Wotan, 'he was lucky. Imagine what it would have been like being married to her. Give me a spear in the small of the back any day.' The Lord of the Ravens shook his head sadly. 'They blame me, of course. They blame me for everything. The only people in the world who aren't entitled to.'

'About the Rhinedaughters,' suggested Loge.

'Ask them to do anything useful, of course, and you get bad temper all day long. No, my family is a great trial to me, and I am a great trial to my family. If I had my time over again . . .'

'The Hoover's broken,' said Waltraute, appearing in the doorway. 'I suppose I'll have to do the stairs with a dustpan and brush.'

'Yes, I suppose you will.' Wotan stood up, his one eye flashing. 'You'll enjoy doing that.'

He strode through the long corridors of Valhalla with Loge trotting at his heels like a terrified whippet, while all around him there came the calls of the Valkyries, informing him of further domestic disasters, until the vaulted ceiling that the Giants had built re-echoed with the sound.

'England, did you say?' whispered Wotan.

'Yes.'

'Oh, good,' said Wotan. 'Let's go there straight away.'

'Mind you,' said Wotan, 'I don't quite know how we're going to tackle this one.'

'Couldn't we just rush him?' Loge suggested. 'I'll hold his arms while you get the Ring off him.'

They stood and looked up at the electrically-operated gates of the Hall. A gardener in a smart new boiler suit walked up to them, holding a rake.

'You can't park there,' he said.

The long, sleek Mercedes limousine was blocking the driveway. Wotan stared at the gardener, who took no notice.

'Move it, or I'll call the police,' said the gardener. 'I've told you once.'

'Certainly, right away,' muttered Loge. There was no point in causing unnecessary trouble. 'Sorry.'

'That's bad,' said Wotan, as they walked up from the village green, where they had parked the car. 'I tried closing up his lungs to make it hard for him to breathe, but it didn't work. We're too near the Ring-Bearer's seat of power to be able to achieve anything by force. I imagine that idiot was under his protection.'

Wotan stopped and studied the gates.

'There's no way through there by violence,' he said. 'We must be clever.'

For some reason or other, Loge had a horrible feeling that by We, Wotan meant him. 'What do you have in mind?' he asked.

'There are many things in the world that mortal men fear more than the Gods,' said Wotan, airily. 'I think it's about time that the Ring-Bearer was brought down to earth. He's a human being, not a God, and he's a citizen of a twentieth-century democracy.' Wotan chuckled. 'The poor bastard.'

Malcolm was feeling happier than he had for some considerable time. He had just had lunch with a remarkably pretty girl, he was going to have lunch with her tomorrow, and, best of all, his secretary had just told him that she was going to take her annual holiday in a week's time. She was, needless to say, going to the Cotswolds. Malcolm thought that they would probably make her an honorary member.

So, when the English Rose came knocking on his door at four o'clock, he expected nothing worse than a recital of her holiday plans. He draped a smile over his face and asked her what he could do for her.

'There's a man downstairs,' she said, 'from the Government.'

Given what he had been doing since he acquired the Ring, it was understandable that Malcolm misunderstood this statement. He expected to find a humble messenger imploring him to take over the reins of State, or at least to accept a peerage. What he found was a sharp-faced individual in a dark grey suit with a briefcase.

'Herr Finger,' said the intruder, 'I'm from Customs and Excise. We're making inquiries about illicit gold dealing.'

For a moment, Malcolm forgot who he had become, and his blood froze. Like all respectable people, he knew that he was guilty of something, although what it was he could not say; and the arrival of a representative of the Main Cop only confirmed his suspicions.

'I don't know what you mean,' he stammered.

'About a month ago, a considerable sum of money in used currency notes was removed from the vaults of the Bank of England. Similar – withdrawals, shall we say? – were made from state banks all over the world. At the same time, large quantities of gold made an inexplicable appearance in the same vaults. Have you any comment, Herr Finger?'

Malcolm was too frightened to speak, and simply shook his head.

'On close examination, the gold was found to be part of a

consignment supplied by a certain . . .' the man paused, as if choosing the right word '. . . a certain underground movement,' he continued, 'to a subversive organisation, based in this country but with international links. This organisation has been secretly undermining the fabric of society for some time, Herr Finger.'

'Has it?' Malcolm's throat was dry.

'It most certainly has. And our investigations have led us to the conclusion . . .'

Malcolm, who for the last twenty-five years had done little in the evenings except watch the television, knew what was coming next. There was no point in running. Faceless men in lounge suits were probably aiming rifles at him at this very moment.

'. . . that you have some connection with this – this subversive ring.'

The word Ring exploded in Malcolm's mind like a bomb. He focused on the intruder's mind, and did not have to read very far.

'*Now* do you have any comment to make, Herr Finger? Or should I say Malcolm Fisher?'

Malcolm leaned back in his chair and smiled serenely.

'If only my mother could see me,' he said, and the serene smile became a grin. 'Chatting like this with a real God.'

'I beg your pardon? Mr Fisher, this is not a laughing matter.'

'You're Loge, aren't you? It's odd. I was frightened of you when I thought you were the taxman, but now you turn out to be a God, I'm not frightened at all.'

'Oh, well,' said Loge, 'I should have known better, I suppose. But Wotan thought it was worth a try.'

'It was,' said Malcolm. 'You had me worried, like I said. What were you going to do?'

'He'll murder me if I go back without it,' said Loge. 'He's got a horrid temper.'

'What can he do to you? You're immortal.'

'That's the trouble.' Loge was trembling. 'If you're

mortal, all they can do to you is kill you. But if you're going to live forever, they can really get you.'

'Surely not?'

'Don't you believe it. He'll turn me into an aquarium, I know he will.'

'I'll get the housekeeper to bring us some tea,' said Malcolm soothingly.

Loge calmed down slightly with some tea inside him, but the cup rattled in the saucer as he held it.

'I was meant to put the frighteners on you,' he said. 'First, I was to be a Customs man, then the VAT inspector, then the Fraud Squad, then MI5. If that didn't work, then I was to be the man from the IPU.'

'What's the IPU?'

'Inexplicable Phenomena Unit. Wotan was sure you'd believe in it. It would be something like all those science fiction films about flying saucers invading the earth, and there's always a secret Government agency that knows all about them but keeps them secret so as not to alarm people. They're the ones who come and zap the Martians in the last reel. And I was going to be them, threatening to zap you. Sometimes I think he lives in a world of his own.'

'He must be a difficult person to work for,' said Malcolm.

'Difficult!' Loge cast his eyes up to the ceiling. 'He's impossible.'

'But I thought you were the clever one,' said Malcolm.

'I used to be, back in the old days when life was much simpler. But progress has left me behind, I'm afraid, and Wotan has got more devious. And he's never forgiven me for the mistake I made in drawing up the contract for Valhalla.'

'Mistake?'

Loge nodded glumly. 'Oh, yes, it was a mistake all right, and I've never been allowed to forget it. A slip of the pen, and now look at me.'

'What sort of a mistake?' asked Malcolm, purely from curiosity.

Loge sighed. 'I might as well tell you. You'll find out sooner or later. The contract with the Giants was that they built us the castle in return for trading concessions in Middle Earth, and the German for "free port" is *freihafen*. But the trouble was,' Loge said, and even after a thousand years he blushed, 'well, my handwriting has never been marvellous, and what I'd written looked more like *Freia zu haben*, which would mean that they would have the Goddess Freia as their reward for that bloody castle. I don't know what you're laughing at. It was a mistake anyone could have made.'

Malcolm, despite his ill-concealed mirth, could sympathise, for his own handwriting was none too good. 'But couldn't you explain the mistake?' he said.

'I did, God knows. But they wouldn't listen, and Wotan had just had a quarrel with Freia and was only too glad to get rid of her. He's always quarrelling with his relatives.'

Again, Malcolm could sympathise. 'Well,' he said, 'at least it explains how that bargain came to be made. I couldn't understand it, the way it is in the books.'

'Now you know.' Loge was depressed again. 'It was only because I suggested this Ring business that he didn't change me into something wet and nasty there and then. And that backfired too – well, you know all about that – and I've been one jump away from metamorphosis ever since.'

Malcolm felt a curious sense of authority, and his tone to Loge was pleasantly patronising. 'Don't worry,' he said, 'I won't let him turn you into anything.'

'And how exactly will you stop him?'

'I don't know,' Malcolm confessed. 'But he can't go throwing his weight about like that any more. He'll just have to face facts, he's had his time.'

Loge raised an eyebrow. 'Don't take this the wrong way,' he said, 'but for someone who was terrified of the Customs inspector a few minutes ago, you're remarkably confident.'

'I know. But that was real life. This is . . . well, it's real life too, but different somehow.' Malcolm was silent for a

103

while, as he tried to work something out in his mind. 'You know how some people are good at some things and bad at others,' he said. 'For instance, some people are marvellous at business or the Stock Exchange or whatever, but they can't change a plug or iron a shirt. Maybe I'm like that. Maybe I'm hopeless at everything except being the master of the Ring, but I'm very good at that. I know how to do it, more or less, and only I can do it, and I'm happy doing it.'

'Are you?'

'Well, no. But I'm no more miserable doing it than doing anything else, plus I can do it well, and I can't do anything else. It's like some people are naturally good singers or snooker players or they can compose music, and they've never tried it so they don't know. And then they do try it, just by accident or for fun, never expecting they'll be any good at it, and there they are. I don't know,' he said despairingly, 'maybe I'm imagining it. Maybe it's so easy any fool can do it. But I'm not afraid any more – not of your lot, anyway.'

Loge stared at him in amazement. 'You've been drinking,' he said at last.

Malcolm shook his head. 'No, I mean it. I may be no good at all at real life, but this sort of thing – you can tell your boss to do his worst and see if I care. I've already seen off Alberich and the Rhinedaughters, and I'll deal with him too, if he makes a nuisance of himself. I mean, what can he do to me? I can understand all languages and read people's thoughts, so I'll always know what's really going on. I can change my shape, so anything he tries to attack me with I can either beat or run away from. And I don't think that's all, either. I don't think he's got any power against the Ring. If he wants to do something and I won't let him, then he can't do it. Stands to reason.'

'How's that?'

'Simple. Unless I do something wrong or think nasty thoughts, nothing unpleasant can happen in the world. So nothing unpleasant can happen to *me*, can it? I'm just as much a citizen of the world as anyone else, so I'm under my own protection.' Malcolm was quite carried away by this train of thought. 'What's that bit in the Bible about He saved others, He couldn't save Himself? You won't catch me falling for that one. And that's why I met that girl,' he went on, more to himself than to Loge. 'Nice things are happening to everyone else, so they're happening to me too.' He laughed for pure joy, and Loge tapped the side of his head.

'You're as bad as he is,' he said. 'Don't say I didn't warn you.'

'Don't worry about a thing,' said Malcolm, grandly. 'Everything will be fine, you'll see.'

Loge rose to his feet. 'I hope you're right,' he said. 'If not, come and feed the ducks on me on Sunday afternoons.'

Wotan leaned back in the driver's seat of the Mercedes, turning over Loge's story in his cavernous mind.

'He's right, up to a point,' said the King of the Gods. 'Like I thought, force and violence are no good, and besides, I'm not sure how far I could take them. I still don't think I could actually take the Ring from him against his will without getting into serious trouble.'

'Who with?'

'Me, in my role as the God of Justice. If I did take it and I found that I wasn't allowed to, I would have to cease to exist. Damn.'

The Sky-God thought hard for a moment, then smiled. He had thought of something. Loge waited impatiently to hear what it was.

'It worked before,' said Wotan quietly. 'So why shouldn't it work again?'

Loge was mystified. 'What?' he asked.

'The Brunnhilde option,' said Wotan. 'Why not?'

'But it didn't work the first time,' Loge said. 'It failed miserably.'

'Because of the Hagen factor and the Siegfried aspect.

And, if we're going to be honest about it, the Brunnhilde aspect, too. But now we're dealing with a different kettle of fish.'

The metaphor made Loge squirm. 'It's a terrible gamble,' he said. 'Don't blame me if . . .'

'As if I would. No, I think I've cracked it. He's just the sort of idiot who'd fall for it.'

'That's true.' Loge began to feel cautiously optimistic. 'Why shouldn't he be his own worst enemy, just like everyone else?'

Malcolm watched the black limousine driving away, and poured himself a small whisky. He was rather worried about what he had said; it was the first time he had ever talked to a God, and perhaps he should have shown more respect. He strolled into the garden, and a blackbird fluttered down and perched in a rose bush beside him.

'Have you seen a white moth with pale blue spots on its wings?' asked the bird.

'No,' replied Malcolm, 'but I've got some peanuts if you're hungry.'

'You can have enough of peanuts,' said the bird. 'Anyway, I wanted that particular moth. We've got people coming round for dinner tomorrow.'

'Good hunting, then,' said Malcolm. 'Try round by the buddleias.'

The bird cocked its head on one side. 'Thanks,' it said. 'Good idea. Oh, and by the way.'

'Yes?'

'Don't underestimate Wotan, whatever you do. There are more ways of killing a cat, you know.'

'What do you mean?'

The bird fluttered its wings. 'Don't ask me, I'm only a bird. Besides, it's my favourite proverb.'

'Hope you find your moth,' said Malcolm.

'So do I,' said the blackbird. 'Good night.'

9

Flosshilde was always beautifully dressed. She had been following fashion since the dawn of time, and her wardrobe occupied the space on the bed of the Rhine between Andernach and Koblenz. Not only did she follow fashion, she led it; she had been wearing figure-of-eight brooches when the Iron Age was still in its infancy, and it was her pioneering work that had given the ladies of sixteenth-century Europe the surcingle. In comparison, she thought, the twentieth century was drab, to say the least. Nevertheless, she had looked out a rather clever lemon-coloured pullover and a pair of black and white striped trousers which had, oddly enough, been in vogue at the height of the Hallstadt Culture. If you keep things long enough, she had learnt by experience, they eventually come back into fashion.

To add the finishing touches, she decorated her ears with Snoopy earrings and slipped over her slim wrist a bracelet of amber which had been given to her by the first King of the Langobards and which looked reasonably like tortoiseshell plastic. She would, she concluded, do.

'Sorry I'm late,' she said, as she sat down beside Malcolm in Carey's.

'You're not,' he replied. 'You're exactly on time.'

'Am I?' Flosshilde looked most surprised. She had always made a habit of being at least five minutes late for everything, especially dates and assignations. If she had subconsciously decided to be punctual, there was cause for concern . . .

107

'I had a visit from Loge yesterday,' Malcolm said.

'Loge?' Flosshilde's blue eyes opened wide. 'What happened?'

'He tried to frighten me, but I soon got rid of him,' Malcolm replied smugly. 'He's not too bad when you get to know him.'

Flosshilde was going to say something about this, but she somehow decided against it. Instead, she smiled.

'I know a funny story about him,' she said.

'Is it the one about the Valhalla contract?'

'Yes,' said Flosshilde, slightly annoyed.

'Tell me anyway,' Malcolm said and, to her surprise, Flosshilde found that she wasn't annoyed any more. She told him the story, and he laughed.

'You tell it better than he does,' he said.

'Of course I do,' said Flosshilde. 'I'm very good at telling stories. Have you heard the one about Hagen and the Steer-Horn?'

The name Hagen made Malcolm feel uncomfortable, and he wondered why she had mentioned it. Perhaps it was a sort of warning. Instinctively, he covered his right hand with his left, so as to hide the Ring.

'Go on,' he said nervously.

As she told the story (which was very funny), Malcolm found himself looking at her rather carefully. He had done this before, of course, for she was well worth looking at, and once Malcolm had accepted that there was a future in looking at her it had become one of his favourite occupations. But he was looking for something else now. She was, after all, one of Them, and he would do well not to forget that. To reassure himself, he flicked through her subconscious mind and was delighted to find that there had been developments. It irritated him that he could not read his own inner thoughts, but he had a fair idea of what they were, on this subject at least. In his life to date, he had met very few girls, and most of those had been friends of his sister Bridget. As a result, he had tended to fall in love with all the rest, just to be on the safe side. Since there had been no risk of the love being returned, this was strictly his own business and nothing to do with anyone else. Only since he had met Flosshilde had he become aware that this was a rather foolish thing to do, and he had been relieved to find that the Rhinedaughter had not inspired the usual romantic daze in him that he knew so well. Instead, once he had got over the shock of seeing what was in her mind and wondering if she could really mean him and not some other Malcolm Fisher, he had carefully considered whether or not he liked her. He did, of course, but that was because she was nice, not just simply because she was there.

Tentatively, he lifted his left hand and used it to pick up his fork. The Ring was visible again, but she did not even look at it. Suddenly, a terrible thought struck Malcolm. Bearing in mind the conclusions he had just come to, what was he supposed to do next?

Flosshilde had seemed rather put out when he had told her that he would be busy for the rest of the day, but the statement had been partially true. There had been a letter from a certain L. Walker, of Lime Place, Bristol, that morning, and it seemed that L. Walker was coming to Combe Hall to catalogue the library.

The library, which was huge and contained no funny books, had come with the Hall when Malcolm bought it, and he had left it alone. Books, the estate agent had told him, provide excellent insulation, and since the heating bills would be very considerable in any event, he might as well leave them there even if he had no intention of ever reading them. Ever since he had moved in, however, the English Rose had been nagging him to have the library professionally catalogued, so that Malcolm would be able to know at a glance what he was missing. He had strenuously resisted these attempts, but he supposed that his secretary had booked L. Walker before she left for her holiday and deliberately not told him.

He drove back to Combe and went into the house. The housekeeper had been lying in wait for him, and he was tempted to make himself invisible before she could persuade him to buy a new vacuum-cleaner – she had been demanding one for weeks, although Malcolm knew perfectly well there were at least four in the house already. Perhaps she was starting a collection. But lately he had felt guilty about avoiding people who were, after all, his employees and only doing their jobs, so he stood his ground, like Leonidas at Thermopylae.

'There's someone to see you,' said the housekeeper.

'Who is it?'

'About the library,' she said. 'From Bristol.'

She made it sound as if Bristol was somewhere between Saturn and Pluto. But to Malcolm, who had been dealing with strangers from Valhalla and Nibelheim for what seemed like years now, Bristol sounded delightfully homely.

'That'll be L. Walker,' he said. 'Where did you put her?'

The housekeeper said the lady was in the drawing-room, and Malcolm had walked away before he thought to ask which one. Eventually, he found the stranger in the Blue drawing-room.

L. Walker was about five feet four, roughly twenty-three years old, with long, dark hair and the face of an angel. Malcolm, who knew exactly what an angel looks like, having turned himself into one during an idle moment, felt a very curious sensation, almost like not being able to breathe properly.

'Herr Finger?' said the girl. 'I'm Linda Walker. I've come to catalogue the library. Ms Weinburger . . .'

'Yes, of course.' Malcolm did not want to hear about the English Rose. He wanted to know why his knees had gone weak, as if he had just been running. There was a long silence while Malcolm tried to regain the use of his mind.

'Could I see the library, perhaps?' said the girl.

'Yes,' Malcolm replied. 'It's through here somewhere.'

He found it eventually, which was good work on his part

considering that he had just been struck by lightning or something remarkably similar. He opened the door and pointed at the rows of books.

'That's it in there,' he said.

'Well,' said the girl, 'I think I'll start work now, if you don't mind. The sooner I start, the sooner I'll be out from under your feet.'

'There's no rush, honestly,' said Malcolm quickly. 'Please take as long as you like.'

The girl looked at him and smiled. Malcolm had come to believe that he was fairly well equipped to deal with smiles, but this was a new sort; not a happy, optimistic smile but a sad, wistful smile. It didn't say, 'Wouldn't it be nice if . . .' like the stock delivery of a Rhinemaiden, but, 'It would have been nice if . . .' which is quite different.

'Thank you,' said the girl, 'but I'd better get on.'

Malcolm began to feel that something he wanted was slipping through his fingers. 'Where are you staying?' he asked.

'At the George and Dragon,' said the girl. 'I hope that's all right. Ms Weinburger booked me in there.'

'You could stay here, if you like. There's masses of room.' As soon as he spoke the words, Malcolm wished he hadn't. There was something about this girl that made him feel like a predator, even though such thoughts had not crossed the threshold of his mind. The girl looked at him for about three-quarters of a second (although it seemed much longer). Then she smiled again, an 'It's hopeless and we both know that, but . . .' sort of a smile.

'I'd like that very much,' she said. 'If you're sure it'd be all right.'

As far as Malcolm was concerned, it could go in the Oxford Dictionary as a definition of all right. 'I'll get the housekeeper to get a room ready,' he said. 'How long will it take you, do you think?'

'About a week,' said the girl, 'if I start today.'

'But aren't you very tired, after your journey? How did you get here, by the way?'

'I got the train to Taunton and the bus to Combe,' said the girl.

Malcolm was shocked to think of a girl like this having to travel by bus and train. He wanted to offer to buy her a car, but she would probably take it the wrong way.

'Did that take long?' A stupid question, and none of his business. Why should he care how long it took? Oddly enough, the girl didn't say that. Instead, she answered the question.

'Oh, about three hours. I missed the connection at Taunton, I'm afraid.'

Try as he might, Malcolm could think of no way of prolonging the conversation. He had no idea what he should say or do next, which was a pity, since he could imagine nothing in the world more important.

'Well,' he said, 'I'd better let you get on, then. See you later.'

He left the library and walked slowly back to the drawing-room, bumping into several pieces of furniture on the way. This was awful, and he could see that plainly enough. Real life had caught up with him at last; not in the form of a Customs man or the Inexplicable Phenomena Unit, which he could probably have dealt with, but the juvenile delinquent with the golden arrows who had been making a dartboard of his heart since his voice had broken. This was no Rhinedaughter out of the world of his own in which he had been living and where he was master, but a fellow human being, a person, a potential source of great unhappiness.

'Oh *God*,' he moaned. 'Not again.'

He sat down on the stairs and looked across at the library door. If he went away, he might miss her coming out, and that would never do. Then it occurred to him that he could make himself invisible and go and watch her cataloguing books, which must surely be the most wonderful sight in the world. He closed his eyes and was lost to sight.

* * *

Beside the unsalubrious waters of the Tone, Flosshilde stood and watched a seagull trying unsuccessfully to catch and eat an abandoned tyre. She knew how it felt, in a way, and out of pure sympathy she smiled at the tyre, which turned itself helpfully into a fish. The seagull, who had known all along that persistence overcomes all obstacles, devoured it thankfully, which was hard luck on the fish but nice for the seagull. You can't please everybody all the time, Flosshilde reflected, and the relevance of this observation to her own case made her thoughtful.

Not that she had any logical reason to be anything but happy; but in matters of happiness, logic plays but a small part. First, it was annoying that Malcolm had preferred to spend the day with a stuffy old librarian than a gorgeous Rhinedaughter. Second, it was annoying that she should be annoyed. In fact, it was the latter irritation that was the worse, or so she hoped. The first unpleasant thing was merely a matter of her vanity (she told herself). The second unpleasant thing might have serious consequences for her career. An enamoured Rhinedaughter, like a blind chauffeur, is unlikely to progress far in her chosen profession. Try as she might, however, she was unable to feel greatly concerned about the prospect, and that was worse still . . .

'Bother,' she said.

Wellgunde, who had been circling slowly under the surface, jumped up onto the bank. 'Get you,' she said. 'All dressed up and nowhere to go.'

Flosshilde put her tongue out, but Wellgunde ignored her. 'I thought you'd have been out with your friend,' she said, shaking the water out of her hair.

'Well, I'm not,' replied Flosshilde.

'Playing hard to get, are you?'

At that particular moment, Flosshilde would have liked to be able to turn her sister into a narrowboat. 'Haven't you got anything better to do?' she said wearily.

'I'm keeping you company,' replied Wellgunde. 'You look as though you could do with cheering up.'

'I'm perfectly cheerful, thank you,' said Flosshilde coldly.

'It must be wonderful to be in love,' cooed Wellgunde. 'I'm terribly jealous.'

'I'm not in any such thing,' snapped her sister. 'But I can understand you being jealous.'

Wellgunde took out a mirror and examined herself lovingly. 'You're only young once, I suppose,' she said. 'You go ahead and enjoy yourself. Don't you worry about us.'

Flosshilde frowned. Sisters can be very annoying at times.

'Don't let it worry you that if you go off with this Ring-Bearer of yours, we'll never get our Ring back ever. Don't let it cross your mind that the Ring is all we've got, since we haven't got dashing boyfriends who have to disguise themselves as other people if they ever want to get anywhere.'

'Don't worry, I won't.'

'We're your sisters, after all. We don't want to stand in your way for a second. And if you think it's worth it, you go ahead. Well, since you're not going to be busy this afternoon, you might put a duster round the riverbed. It was your turn yesterday, but you were out.'

'Oh, go away,' said Flosshilde rudely.

'I'm going,' said Wellgunde placidly. 'I only popped up to tell you that while you've been moping about, we've been working.'

'I thought you said you were going to leave him alone.'

'We haven't been persecuting your precious darling, if that's what you mean. We've been chatting with Thought and Memory.'

'How fascinating.'

'Yes, it was rather. Apparently, they've been watching Combe Hall all day, and your friend was having ever such a long chat with an extremely nice-looking girl.'

Any doubts Flosshilde might have had about her feelings for Malcolm were dispelled by this news. She went as white as a sheet.

'Of course, they can't read his thoughts because he's the Ring-Bearer, so they can't be sure, but to listen to those two you don't have to be able to read thoughts to see what your friend thinks of his new friend. Written all over his silly face, they said.'

'That's nice for him,' Flosshilde said, very quietly.

'Well,' said Wellgunde, 'it's not so nice for us, is it? What if he gives her the Ring? Where would we all be then?'

Flosshilde said something extremely disrespectful about the Ring and dived into the Tone, leaving Wellgunde looking very pleased with herself. Perhaps, mused the eldest of the Rhinedaughters, she hadn't told her sister the whole truth, but then, she had gone off in a huff without giving her a chance. Her conscience was clear . . .

After spending the whole afternoon lugging heavy books about, Malcolm imagined, she would be sure to want a rest and possibly a drink. He wished he could have helped her, but that would have looked pointed, since one does not buy a dog and bark oneself. Besides, if he had materialised out of thin air and said 'Can I carry that for you?' she would probably have had a fit; another of the problems associated with dealing with a real person.

She was certainly conscientious, and Malcolm admired that, but she had carried on with her work for a very long time. When finally she seemed to be about to call it a day, Malcolm transported himself back to the stairs and wondered what on earth he was to do next. It seemed like hours before the library door opened, and still he hadn't thought of anything. He stood up quickly, and tried to look as if he was just passing.

'Finished for the day?' he asked.

'Yes, thanks,' she said, and smiled again. This smile, a sort of 'If only . . . but no' smile, wiped Malcolm's mind clean of thoughts and words, and he stood gawping at her as if she was the one who had suddenly appeared out of thin air.

115

'Are you sure it's no trouble for me to stay here?' she said.

'No, of course not. I told the housekeeper to phone the George and Dragon.'

'Thank you, then,' she said.

'I took your suitcase up to your room,' he went on, as if this act had been comparable to saving her from drowning. 'And I've told the cook you'll be having dinner . . . If that's all right, I mean.'

That was not how he had meant to suggest that she should have dinner with him. He had wanted to suggest it casually. He had wanted many things in his life, and got very few of them. But the girl did not seem to mind. She said, 'Are you sure that's all right?' and Malcolm felt a tiny flicker of impatience within his raging heart, but it passed very quickly.

'It must be nice having a cook,' she said.

Malcolm felt the need to defend himself against a charge of hedonism. 'I'm afraid I'm a dreadful cook,' he said. 'And she sort of came with the place.'

The girl said nothing, and Malcolm forced some more words into his mouth, grabbing the first ones that came to hand.

'You know how it is,' he burbled, 'these great big houses.'

Utter drivel of course, but she seemed not to notice. 'Yes,' she said, 'we used to live in a huge old house. It was dreadfully difficult to keep it clean and warm.'

She seemed unwilling to expand on this point, and they walked on in silence. Malcolm had no idea where they were going, but that did not seem to matter very much.

'Was it as big as this? Your house, I mean.' Any more of this, Malcolm thought, and I shall bite my tongue off.

'Yes,' said the girl. 'It kept me and my sisters very busy.'

'You've got sisters, then?' he went on, as if that were the most remarkable thing that he had ever heard.

'Eight,' said the girl. 'It's a large family. Are you *sure* it's all right me staying to dinner? I mean, you haven't got people coming or anything?'

'No,' Malcolm said, 'really. Shall we go and sit in the drawing-room?'

The girl was silent, as if thinking this over very carefully. 'Yes,' she said at last.

It was at this point that it occurred to Malcolm that he hadn't read her thoughts, to see if by any chance they resembled his, no matter how remotely. But he found that he didn't want to. It seemed somehow indecent, for she was not a God or a Rhinedaughter, but a human being. Besides, if she wasn't thinking along the same lines as he was, he really didn't want to know.

'You speak English very well,' she said, as Malcolm eventually found the drawing-room.

'Thank you,' Malcolm said, deeply touched, and only just managed to stop himself from returning the compliment. 'I went to school in England,' he said, truthfully. 'Can I get you a drink?'

'No, thank you,' said the girl, looking down at her feet.

'Are you sure?'

'Well, if you're sure . . .'

Malcolm was sure, but he felt it would be superfluous to say so. 'What can I get you?' he asked.

'A small sherry, please.'

Malcolm poured out a small sherry – very small, as it turned out, for he did not want her to think he was trying to get her drunk. 'Is that enough?' he asked.

'That's fine.' Another smile, this time a 'We can't go on like this, you know' smile.

'So how long have you been cataloguing?'

'About two years,' said the girl. That seemed to put the seal on that particular subject.

'I suppose it's like being a librarian,' Malcolm went on, and he reckoned that digging peat was probably easier work than making conversation under these circumstances. The girl agreed that it was very like being a librarian.

'How long have you lived here?' she asked, and Malcolm found that he could not remember. He had to think hard before he replied. Afterwards, there was a long silence, during which the girl drank a quarter of her small sherry. The temptation to read her thoughts was very strong, but Malcolm resisted it. It wouldn't be fair.

'So how do you set about cataloguing a library?' he asked. The girl told him, and that took up at least three minutes, during which time Malcolm was able to collect what remained of his thoughts. Summoning up all his powers of imagination, he compiled a list of questions and topics which might, with a great deal of luck, get them through dinner.

In the event, they nearly did, although Malcolm had to use a great deal of ingenuity. Why did he find it so easy to talk to Flosshilde, who was only a friend, and so difficult to keep a conversation going with the most wonderful person in the world? There was only one topic that he couldn't mention; on the other hand, it was the one topic he did want to discuss with her. Instead, they mostly seemed to talk about libraries, a subject that Malcolm had never given much consideration to in the past. At about half-past nine, even this theme collapsed into silence, and Malcolm resigned himself to yet another disappointment. The girl was obviously nervous and ill at ease; scarcely to be wondered at. She had come here to do a straightforward job of work, the job she had trained to do and at which she was no doubt highly competent, and instead of being allowed to go to a comfortable hotel where she could take her shoes off and read a good book, she had been compelled to listen to his inane ramblings. She must think he was mad. Certainly, she wouldn't be there in the morning. At first light, she would unlock her door and make a run for it, or climb out of the window down a rope of sheets. It was all unbearably sad, and as a human being he was a complete and utter failure. He had made the mistake of treating a normal, grown-up woman from the twentieth century as if she was something out of a romantic story, and he deserved all the heartbreak he was undoubtedly going to get.

'I expect you're very tired,' he said abruptly, 'after the journey and a hard day's work. I'll show you to your room.'

They tracked up the stairs in silence. It was still light outside, but she could read a book or something until it was time to go to sleep. At least he wasn't sending her to bed without any supper.

'Good night, then,' she said, and she smiled at him for the last time that day. It was a smile you could take a photograph by, and it said, 'I like you very much and it's a pity you think I'm so boring, but there we go.' The door closed in front of the embers of it, and Malcolm stood in the hall opening and shutting his eyes. To hell with being fair. He located her thoughts and read them. Then he read them again, just to be sure. Then he read them again, because he liked them so much.

'Well I'm damned,' he said slowly to himself. 'Well I never.'

Then he went to bed.

The two ravens floated down and perched on the roof of the Mercedes. Wotan put his head out of the window and said 'Well?'

'They've gone to bed,' said Thought.

'Separately,' said Memory.

'But not to worry,' said Thought. 'She's doing all right.'

Wotan frowned. 'But he can read her thoughts,' said Wotan. 'He'll just look into her mind and then it'll be all over. He'll chuck her out so fast she'll bounce all the way down the drive.'

Memory chuckled. 'I wouldn't worry on that score,' he croaked. 'He's dead meat. Head over heels.'

'And even if he does,' said his partner, 'he'll only make things worse for himself. I had a quick look myself.'

'Oh.' Wotan was baffled. 'You can't mean she fancies him?'

'Something rotten,' said Thought. 'You wouldn't read about it.'

'Oh, that's *marvellous*,' Wotan said, disgusted. 'Now I'll never get the perishing thing back.'

'Relax,' said Memory. 'You know her. Duty must come first, even if it means betraying the man she truly loves.'

'Especially if it means betraying the man she loves,' said Thought. 'She's a real chip off the old block, that girl.'

Wotan was forced to agree. Of all his eight surviving daughters, the Valkyrie Ortlinde most resembled her father in her capacity for self-torture. She would revel in it. Most of all, she would enjoy blaming him afterwards.

'We've cracked it,' said Wotan.

10

Alberich loathed travelling by air. This was partly the natural prejudice of one who had lived most of his life underground, partly because the food that they serve you on little plastic trays with hollow mouldings to hold the ketchup gave him violent indigestion. But he was a businessman, and businessmen have to travel on aircraft. Since there seemed to be no prospect of progress in his quest for the Ring, he had thought it would be as well if he went back to Germany for a week to see what sort of a mess his partners were making of his mining consultancy. He had no interest in the work itself, but it provided his bread and butter; if it did not exactly keep the wolf from the door, it had enabled him to have a wolf-flap fitted so that the beast could come in and out without disturbing people.

As luck would have it, he had been given a seat by the window, and he looked aimlessly out over the world that by rights should have been his. If he had had any say in its running, there would have been fewer cities and more forests. He let his attention wander for a moment.

Something was tapping on the window. He looked round, and saw a slightly bedraggled raven pecking at the thick Perspex with its beak. A second raven was beating the air furiously with its wings, trying to hover and fly at the speed of sound at the same time.

'What do you want?' he mouthed through the window.

The raven pecked away vigorously, and Alberich felt slightly nervous. If the stupid bird contrived to break the window, he would be sucked out into space. 'Go away,' he mouthed, and made shooing gestures with his fingers.

'Forget it,' Memory shrieked through the rushing wind. 'He can't hear a word you're saying.'

But Thought was nothing if not persistent. With his beak, he pecked a series of little marks onto the Perspex. When he was finished, Alberich was able to make out the words, 'Wotan says stay out of England,' written back to front on the pane. He nodded to the ravens to acknowledge the message, and they wheeled away exhausted. Alberich pondered this warning for a moment, then looked at his watch. They were due to land in Frankfurt in half an hour.

At Frankfurt Airport, he telephoned his partner.

'Dietrich?' he said. 'It's Hans. Look, I'm at Frankfurt now, but I've got to go back to England right away. There's a flight in three hours. Can you bring me some clean shirts and the papers on the Nigerian project?'

'What have you got to go back for?'

'What's that? Oh, would you believe I left my briefcase behind? With all the things I need for the Trade Fair?'

'Can't they send it on?'

'It'd take too long. I'm going back.'

'Fancy forgetting your briefcase.'

'I'm only human,' Alberich lied. 'Don't forget the shirts.'

To his surprise, Malcolm had managed to get some sleep, but he was awake by six. He went through the events of the previous day in his mind, trying to reassure himself that it had all happened. Something inside him told him that this strange happiness was bound to end in tears, but he put that down to his natural pessimism. Besides, there was one sure way of knowing whether things were all right or not.

He tuned his mind in to the early morning news and was reassured. No disasters had afflicted the world during the last day, although there had been one strange occurrence.

A farmer from the small village of Combe in Somerset had been out shooting rabbits at a quarter to ten last night, and had seen his ten-acre field of wheat change before his eyes into ten acres of roses, peonies, narcissi, daffodils and tulips. The farmer, a Mr William Ayres of Combe Hill Farm, attributed this extraordinary mutation to a leak from the nearby Hinckley Point nuclear power station, although no such leak had as yet been confirmed by the CEGB . . .

Malcolm blinked, and for a moment was concerned. But Mr Ayres was bound to be insured, and even if he wasn't, he could pick the flowers and use them to decorate the church for his daughter's wedding. Malcolm laughed. He bore the Ayres family, both its present and prospective members, no ill will at all, and that was surely a good thing for the world.

It occurred to him that he had forgotten to tell the girl when breakfast would be ready. He jumped out of bed, thought up a light blue shirt and a pair of cream corduroy trousers, and transported himself across the house. As he passed the library, he heard cataloguing noises. Although it was only half-past six, the girl was working already. He listened carefully for her thoughts, and a tender smile hitched up the ends of his mouth. She was throwing herself into her work to take her mind off the sad feelings of longing in her heart. A soppy girl, Malcolm could not help thinking, but none the worse for that. He opened the library door and went in.

'You're up early,' he said.

'I hope I didn't disturb you,' said the girl anxiously.

'Not at all,' Malcolm replied. 'I'm usually awake by this time. Would you like some breakfast?'

After the inevitable 'If you're sure' ritual, she agreed to have a cup of coffee and a slice of toast, and Malcolm hurried down to the kitchen. The coffee machine seemed to take for ever, as did the toaster, but eventually he got what he wanted out of both of them and carried the tray up to the library. In his mind he tried to rehearse some way of bringing the conversation round to the issues he wanted to raise, but he had to give up the attempt. He would think of something when the time came, and he did not want to rush something as important as this, even if the result was a foregone conclusion.

Let other pens dwell on joy and happiness. It is enough to record that Malcolm hijacked a discussion on card-indexes and used it to convey his message. Although he could read the girl's thoughts and so avoid all misunder-standings, he still found it heavy going, and heard himself using words and phrases that would have seemed excess-ively sentimental in *True Love* magazine; but everyone has a right to make fools of themselves once in their lives. The main thing was that everything was going to be all right now, and he had managed to persuade her of this. She had seemed rather diffident at first, but he had got so used to her saying, 'Are you sure you don't mind?' and, 'If you're sure it's no trouble,' that he took no notice of her words and simply watched her thoughts going round, like the figures on a petrol pump. When the appropriate reading came up, he took her hand and squeezed it gently. Through the snowstorm of emotions that raged around him, he heard a tinkling sound, like a coin dropping on the floor. Suddenly this seemed very important, and he looked down. On the polished wooden floor he saw the Ring, which had some-how slipped off his finger. He felt a sudden urge to give it to her; for what better gift could there be than the whole world?

She was still holding his hand, tightly and trustingly, so that it would be incredibly churlish of him to do anything except sit absolutely still and be loved. There was also a particularly fine smile going on, and he let the Ring lie there until it was over. Just to be sure, however, he covered the Ring with his foot.

Everything that needed saying had now been said, and it was obviously the time for action: a kiss, or something of that sort. But Malcolm could not bring himself to initiate such a move, although he could not imagine why. 'One thing at a time,' whispered a voice in his brain. 'Let's not get carried away.' So he contented himself with putting his arm tenderly round her shoulders, and suggesting that they go for a walk in the garden. For once, the girl did not ask him if he was sure that would be no bother, and they stood up, still entwined.

'Just a moment,' Malcolm said. 'Don't go away.'

He stooped down swiftly and picked up the Ring. After a moment's hesitation, he pushed it back onto his finger. It felt loose and uncomfortable.

'So how did you get her to agree to it?' Loge said. 'It must have been difficult.'

'Not really,' said Wotan. 'There was one of those grim silences we know so well in our family, then she said "If you insist," and there we were. I was amazed, as you can imagine. I'd thought up all sorts of arguments – you always said you wanted to work in the family business, it'll get you out of the house, a change is as good as a rest, that sort of thing – and I didn't have to use any of them. Women are strange creatures.'

'Are you sure she's up to it?'

'Positive. You've only seen her in the domestic mode, nagging and persecuting.'

'Which one was it again?'

'Ortlinde. She's the best-looking, and the droopiest. Mind you, with eight of them, I tend to get them mixed up. Maybe I should get them wearing numbers on their backs like footballers. I think Ortlinde's the second from youngest. Fancy another?'

'No, thanks, I'm driving.'

'So am I, but who cares? This is something to celebrate.' Wotan pulled open the drinks cabinet behind the front seat and took out a bottle of schnapps. 'Here's to two birds with one stone. I get control of the Ring and shot of a dopey daughter at the same time.'

'I hate to say this . . .' said Loge.

'I know, I know, it didn't work before and all the rest of it. But that was different.'

'Not so different.' Loge knew he was pushing his luck, but it had to be said. Besides, if it all went wrong, Wotan would be so furious that he would be lucky to get away with being turned into a trout hatchery. 'After all, Siegfried was roughly the same sort of proposition. He'd never had a girl before, either.'

'Siegfried wasn't a drip,' said Wotan crisply. 'This one is. So's she. She's so wet you could grow cress on her.'

'She didn't strike me as wet the other morning.'

'Ah,' said Wotan, 'that's different. That's her complicated little psyche belting away, that is. You see, my daughters are all the same. The way they see it, I've ruined their lives for them by making them stay at home in that bloody great house, stunting their emotional growth and all the rest of it, when they should have gone out into the world and had a good time. And you can see their point, I suppose. That house is a liability.' Wotan scowled at the very thought of it, and the first drops of rain started to fall. 'It's difficult to explain my family to a normal, sane person, but I think it goes something like this. They've been cooped up in Valhalla ever since their mother left, with nothing to do but be resentful and tell themselves how inadequate and unlovable they are, and how nobody could ever be interested in them because of their stunted personalities (stunted by me, it goes without saying). And they take all this out on their poor old dad by making his life almost as miserable as their own, in the tried and tested way you saw the other day.'

Loge had been nodding his head and making sympathetic noises until he felt quite dizzy. He didn't want to hear any of this, but Wotan seemed determined to tell him. A combination of schnapps and relief was making him unwind, although whether he would be any safer to be employed by unwound than tensed up remained to be seen. Rattlesnakes, Loge remembered, usually unwind just before they bite.

'So at home they really let fly. Not that we have long, earnest conversations about the state of our tortured personalities, thank God. No, they've decided that they can't talk to me, I'm delighted to say, and so what they do is they sublimate it all – I think that's the right word, isn't it? – into endless domestic trivia, like who had the Sellotape last and how can you expect me to find things if you will insist on moving them. But put them down in the outside world, and they turn into fluffy little bunnies, wouldn't say boo to a goose, you know the sort of thing. I don't know which is worse, actually. At least they keep the place clean. Anyway, no self-confidence is the root of it all, so if our Ring-Bearer can convince Ortlinde that he's serious about her and that somebody really loves her in spite of everything, he'll need a crowbar to get her off him. Serve the idiot right, that would.'

'But if she hates you so much, what makes you think she'll get the Ring for you? Won't she just go off with her Redeemer and leave you to get on with it?'

'That was worrying me, I must admit, but when I thought it over, I saw just how clever I'd been,' said Wotan smugly. 'The fact that she really does love him in her own, unique, screwed-up way means she can't fail. You see, the last thing my daughter wants is to be happy. She'd hate it. No, what she wants is to be finally, definitively *un*happy, and for it all to be my fault. It'd finally confirm all her dearest illusions about how her life has been ruined. People like that would far rather be right than happy. No, she'll get that Ring if it kills her.'

Loge wiped his forehead with his hand, and wished that he could go away and do something less stressful for a change, such as drive the chariot of the Sun or make the crops grow. But that was out of the question.

'The only thing that could go wrong is if he finds out who she really is,' Wotan said, pouring himself another drink.

127

'But my guess is that he won't want to find out, so unless somebody tells him, he won't work it out for himself. I think he's just as bad as she is. In fact, they're perfectly suited to each other. Who knows, they may even stick together after she's got the Ring off him, and I'll never have to see her ever again. Wouldn't that be perfect? Then there would only be seven of them, one for every day of the week. But it's unlikely,' he added sadly. 'Like I said, she'd go mad if she were happy.'

The rain had stopped, and Loge deduced that Wotan was in a good mood for once. That removed the immediate threat of transformation, but he still felt uneasy. Over the last few thousand years, Loge had found that Wotan's good moods always tended to come before periods of universal misery.

'So what do we do now?' he asked.

'Leave her to it,' said Wotan, leaning back in his seat. 'I always knew she'd come in useful one day.'

Love, the songwriter says, is the sweetest thing, and too many sweet things can make you feel slightly sick. But Malcolm had got through the endearments and sweet nothings stage quite safely, and had finally got the girl to tell him all about herself. She had not wanted to, and as he listened to the story that eventually came pouring out, he could quite understand why. Not that he was bored; but an overdose of tragedy can cause roughly the same symptoms as boredom, such as a strong desire to change the subject. That, however, would not be tactful. He only hoped that he would not be called upon to give an equally full account of himself, which might call for more inventiveness than he felt himself capable of.

'You see,' said the girl, 'none of us could ever really *talk* to my father, and my father could never really *talk* to us, so that in the end I found I couldn't even talk to my sisters. We all just bottled it all up inside ourselves, really, until we

128

wanted to hit out at each other. But we couldn't, because of not being able to talk. Do you see what I'm getting at?'

'Sort of.'

'And it was obvious that my father was absolutely heart-broken when my mother left him. He tried to put a brave face on it, of course, but we all knew that she had let him down as well as letting us down, and that somehow we had let him down as well. And, of course, he feels that he's let us down, and so now we can't communicate at all.'

'That's dreadful,' Malcolm said, wishing he hadn't raised the subject in the first place. It was obviously very painful for her to talk about her problems like this, and he hoped that she would stop and not upset herself further. But no such luck.

'And we could all see how much of a disappointment we were to him. He wanted us to have careers and achieve something in the world, but we knew we couldn't leave him like that after my mother had left him, because he would feel left out and that would be awful.'

'But you've got a career,' said Malcolm, brightly.

The girl looked startled, as if she had made a mistake. 'Well, sort of,' she said. 'But it's not a proper one.'

'But you don't live in the family house any more, do you?'

'Yes. No. Well, sort of. I share this flat, but I go home a lot too.'

The girl stopped talking and stared at her shoes. They were sensible shoes and had seen many seasons, like her sensible tweed skirt and her honest cream pullover. Her mother had probably bought them for her, Malcolm thought, just before she left.

'Well,' he said, trying to sound cheerful, 'you've got me to look after you now.'

They sat down on a bench and looked out over the park. It was a beautiful morning, although there had been one brief shower, and as soon as all the tragic stories had been got over with, it would all be perfect.

'What do you like doing?' Malcolm asked.

'Oh, I don't know really.' She thought about it for a long time. 'Walking, I suppose. And I quite like my work. Well, no, I don't really, but it's better than nothing.'

'Let's go for a stroll by the river,' Malcolm said firmly.

They walked in silence for a while, and stopped to admire the view of Farmer Ayres' prodigious crop of assorted flowers. In the distance, a BBC camera crew were unrolling miles of flex, so it would probably all be on the 9 O'Clock News that evening. Malcolm wanted to tell her that he had laid the flowers on for her benefit, to show how much he loved her, but he could not think of a way of explaining it all.

'Who's that girl on the river bank waving at you?'

Malcolm followed her finger and recognised Flosshilde. His heart fell. 'That's just a friend of mine,' he said. 'No-one important.'

'I think she wants to say something to you . . . Oh.'

Malcolm could have sworn that she had recognised Flosshilde, but that was obviously impossible, so he did not even bother to check her thoughts. He wanted to walk away and pretend he hadn't seen the Rhinedaughter, for he could not be bothered with her just now. After all, she was a very pretty girl, and Linda might jump to quite the wrong conclusions. Unfortunately, it was too late now. He put his arm around Linda's shoulders rather as a Roman legionary might have raised his shield before facing an enemy, as Flosshilde ran across to join them.

'Hello,' said the Rhinedaughter, and there was something very strange about her manner. 'Hope you don't mind, but I've been for a swim in your river.'

Nervously, Malcolm introduced her to the girl. Flosshilde looked at Malcolm for a moment, then turned and smiled radiantly at the girl, so that for an instant Malcolm was convinced that something terrible was going to happen. But nothing did, and Malcolm reassured himself that he must have been imagining it. For her part, Flosshilde

130

looked very slightly disappointed, although Malcolm could not think why.

'Don't I know you from somewhere?' Flosshilde asked. 'Your face is very familiar.'

'I don't think so,' said the girl, nervously. She was obviously very shy.

'Must be my imagination, then. Well, I must be going. Oh, and I won't be able to make lunch tomorrow. Sorry.'

'Some other time, then,' said Malcolm. 'See you.'

'I expect so,' said the Rhinedaughter. 'Have fun.'

She ran lightly down to the river and dived in. For some reason, the girl did not seem surprised by this, and Malcolm was relieved that he would not have to try and find some explanation. He dismissed Flosshilde from his mind.

The Rhinedaughter circled for a few minutes under the surface, then slowly paddled upstream to a deep pool where she knew she could not be seen. It had been pointless trying to turn the woman into a frog; the daughters of Wotan are not so lightly transformed. At least she had given the Valkyrie notice that she had a fight on her hands.

It was all very well saying that, but Flosshilde had no stomach for a fight. It was inconceivable that Malcolm didn't know who she was or what she was likely to be after, and if he was so much in love that he was prepared to take the risk . . . After all, he had apparently been prepared to take a similar risk with her before the Valkyrie showed up, and obviously he had not been in love then, just lonely. And any fool could see that Ortlinde was completely smitten, so it seemed likely that she too had given up hope of getting the Ring. After all, Malcolm was in a unique position to know what was going on inside her head. So he could take care of himself.

Vanity, said Flosshilde to herself, and wounded pride, that was all it was. That anyone could prefer a stuffy old

Valkyrie to her was naturally hard for her to believe, but Malcolm obviously did, and that was all there was to it.

From the cover of a small boulder, she peered out. The Young Couple were kissing each other rather awkwardly under the shade of an oak tree. Flosshilde shrugged her shoulders and slid back into the water, as graceful as an otter. Beside her, she was aware of her sisters, swimming lazily in the gentle current.

'Told you so,' said Wellgunde.

'I couldn't care less,' said Flosshilde. 'And if you say one word about the Ring, I'll break your silly neck.'

'Wouldn't dream of it, would we?' replied Wellgunde smugly.

'I'm bored with England,' said Flosshilde suddenly, as they reached the head of the Tone. 'Why don't we go back home?'

'What a good idea,' said Woglinde. 'Let's do that.'

11

At Valhalla the Wednesday afternoon General Meeting of
the Aesir, or Company of Gods, is presided over by Wotan
himself. At these meetings, the lesser divinities – thunder-
spirits, river-spirits, cloud-shepherds, Valkyries, Norns,
nixies, powers, thrones, ettins and fetches – have an opportunity to bring to Wotan's attention any matters which they
feel require action on his part, and receive their instructions
for the next seven days. There is also a general discussion
on future strategy and a long-range weather forecast.

Loge, as secretary to the Company, had the unenviable
task of keeping the minutes of each meeting and presenting
the agenda. At the meeting that immediately followed the
Ring-Bearer's entrapment by the Valkyrie Ortlinde, he
found himself having to reorganise the entire programme
to give enough time for a thorough discussion, only to find
that the discussion that followed was over much sooner
than he had anticipated. There were votes of thanks from
the Company to Ortlinde and Wotan, which were duly
entered in the records, and Waltraute inquired how long
Ortlinde was likely to be away and who was supposed to do
her share of the housework while she was absent. Loge was
then compelled to proceed to Any Other Business with well
over an hour of the scheduled time still to go.

'I would like to bring to the Chairman's attention the fact
that the light-bulb on the third-floor landing of the main
staircase of Valhalla has gone again, and I would request
him to replace it immediately,' said Schwertleite, 'before
someone trips over and breaks their neck.'

'That's not nearly as dangerous as the carpet on the back stairs,' said Grimgerde. 'I've asked you hundreds of times to nail it down properly, but nobody ever listens to a word I say.'

Loge was writing furiously. All the minutes of meetings had to be made in runes, which cannot be written quickly.

'May I suggest,' said Wotan, grimly attempting to make himself heard, 'that this is neither the time nor the place . . .'

'Next time you stub your toe in the dark because you couldn't be bothered to replace a light-bulb . . .'

Wotan put his hands in front of his one eye and groaned audibly. 'We were discussing the Ring,' he muttered.

'And please don't put your elbows on the table,' interrupted the Valkyrie Helmwige. 'I spent the whole morning trying to get it looking respectable after you spilt coffee all over it.'

Wotan made a vague snarling noise at the back of his throat. 'This is a meeting of the Aesir,' he growled, 'and I would ask you to behave in an appropriate manner.'

'While we're on the subject,' retorted his daughter, the Driver of the Spoil, 'you might try dressing in an appropriate manner. Why you insist on wearing the same shirt three days in a row . . . How am I expected to get the collars clean?'

'Any other business,' Wotan said, but his growl was more like a whimper.

'You've got whole drawers full of shirts you never wear,' said Grimgerde, with a world of reproach in the deep pools of her blue eyes. She hadn't had a new shirt, or a new anything, for four hundred and twenty years, but she didn't complain. She never went anywhere anyway.

'I shall wear what the hell I like when I like,' said Wotan, and what had intended to be authority when the words passed his vocal cords was definitely petulance when the sounds emerged through the gate of his teeth. 'Now, can we please . . .'

A general baying of Valkyries drowned out the voice of the Sky-God, and Loge stopped trying to keep the minutes of the meeting. Over the centuries, he had evolved his own shorthand for the inevitable collapse into chaos that rounded off each Wednesday afternoon in the Great Hall. He sketched in a succession of squiggles under the last intelligible remark he had been able to record and began drawing sea-serpents.

The discussion had moved on to the topic of leaving the tops off jars when a rock-troll, who had been thoroughly enjoying the conflicts of his betters, noticed something out of the corner of one of his eyes. He nudged the middle-aged Norn with mouse-blond hair who was knitting beside him, and they turned and stared at the doorway of the Hall. One by one, the minor deities, then the Vanir, then the High Gods themselves abandoned the debate and gazed in astonishment at the three rather pretty girls who had wandered in through the Gates of Gylfi.

It was at least a thousand years since the Rhine-daughters, who were responsible for the noblest river in Europe, had attended a Wednesday afternoon meeting. No-one except Wotan and Loge could remember exactly why they had stopped coming. Some said that they had been expelled for flirting with the cloud-shepherds at the time of the Great Flood. Others put it down to the girls' natural frivolity and apathy. Wotan and Loge knew that the river-spirits had walked out in tears after the stormy debate that followed the theft of the Ring from Alberich and had not been back since, although both Gods correctly attributed this continued absence to forgetfulness rather than actual principle.

'Well I never!' whispered the Norn to the rock-troll. 'Look who it is!'

The rock-troll nodded his head. Since he had been created out of solid granite at the dawn of time, this manoeuvre required considerable effort on his part, but he felt it was worth it. 'It's the Girls,' he hissed through his adamantine teeth.

It was Wotan himself who broke the silence. 'What the hell do you want?' he snapped.

'We just thought we'd pop our heads round and say hello,' said Wellgunde sweetly. 'It's been simply ages.'

The silence gave way to a hubbub of voices, as each immortal greeted the long-lost members of their Company. Most vociferous were a group of cloud-shepherds who, several centuries before, had arranged to meet the Rhinedaughters for a picnic at the place which has since become Manchester, and who had been waiting there ever since. Only the Valkyries and their father seemed less than delighted to see the Rhinedaughters back again. Wotan suspected that he knew the reason for their visit, while his daughters felt sure that the river-spirits hadn't wiped their feet before coming into the Hall.

'So,' said Wotan, when the noise had subsided, 'what have you been doing all these years?'

'Sunbathing, mostly,' said Woglinde truthfully. 'Doesn't time fly when you're having fun?'

'It's all right for some,' whispered the Norn to the troll. But the troll seemed uneasy. 'Something's going to happen,' he said, and he sniffed loudly, as if trying to identify some unfamiliar smell.

'Is that all?' laughed Wotan, nervously jovial. 'Or have you been doing any work?'

'Depends on what you call work,' replied Wellgunde. 'The river sort of runs itself really. But we have been looking at other rivers to see if we can pick up any hints.'

'Sort of an exchange visit,' said Woglinde, helpfully.

'For example,' continued Wellgunde, 'we visited a river called the Tone in England. Not very helpful, I'm afraid.'

'But guess who we bumped into while we were over there,' cooed Woglinde. 'Go on, guess.'

'I hate guessing,' said Wotan irritably, and he picked up a document and began to study it diligently. Since he was to all intents and purposes omnipotent, it was not surprising that he could read a sheet of paper that was palpably the wrong way up.

'Ortlinde, that's who,' said Flosshilde, who had not spoken before. Wotan made no reply, being obviously engrossed in his document. Suddenly, Flosshilde smiled at the papers in his hand, which turned into a small dragon. Wotan dropped it with a start, and it crawled away under the table. 'Now what on earth was she doing there?'

The Norn had covered her eyes. She was fond of the Rhinedaughters, with whom she had spent many hours exchanging gossip, and Flosshilde's conjuring trick, performed in front of so many witnesses, was as clear a case of treasonable assault on the King of the Gods as one could hope to find. The penalty for this offence was instant metamorphosis, usually into a bush of some kind, and it was common knowledge that Wotan had been desperate for some pretext for getting rid of the Rhinedaughters ever since they had first emerged from the waters of their native river. Slowly, the Norn lowered her hands. The Girls were still there, still in human shape.

'I'll tell you, shall I?' continued Flosshilde. 'She was there trying to get the Ring-Bearer to give her our Ring, which you should have given back to us a thousand years ago. So will you please tell her to stop it and go away?'

The Norn covered her eyes again, but she need not have bothered. Wotan simply looked away and threw a piece of cheese to the small dragon, which had curled up on his lap.

'If you don't,' said Flosshilde, clear without being shrill, 'we'll tell him who she is. Are you listening?'

There was a terrible silence. Never before had anyone, mortal or immortal, dared to threaten the Lord of Tempests in the Hall of his stronghold. Even the rock-troll held his breath, and the beating of his basalt heart was the only audible sound in the whole assembly. Wotan sat motionless for a moment, then rose sharply to his feet, sending the small dragon scampering for the safety of a coffee-table. He looked the Rhinedaughter in the eye, and the Norn held her breath. Then Wotan shook his head in disbelief, and marched out of the Hall.

'*Not* across the floor I've spent all morning polishing,' wailed the Valkyrie Gerhilde, but her father took no notice. The meeting broke up in disorder, and the troll and the Norn hurried off to the Mortals' Bar for a much-needed drink.

'I dunno,' said the rock-troll. 'I've never seen the like.'

'He just sat there,' said the Norn.

'Who did?'

'Wotan. When Flossie turned that paper into a dragon. It's Kew Gardens for her, I thought, but he just sat there. Didn't do a thing.'

'I didn't mean that,' said the rock-troll. 'I meant the other thing.'

The Norn wasn't listening. 'What I want to know is,' she continued, 'who is bluffing who? Is it the Girls bluffing Wotan, or Wotan bluffing the Girls, or are they all at it?'

The troll frowned and scratched his head, producing a sound like two millstones. 'What are you on about?' he asked.

'You *are* a slowcoach, aren't you? If the Girls wanted to stop Ortlinde from nobbling the Ring-Bearer, why didn't they just tell him who she was, instead of coming here and making threats to Wotan?'

The troll thought about this for a moment, then nodded his head. He was not so grey as he was granite-looking, and he could see that there was indeed an inconsistency.

'What I think,' said the Norn excitedly, 'is that the Ring-Bearer already knows who Ortlinde is, and he couldn't care less. They've tried telling him, and he doesn't want to know.'

'How do you make that out?' asked the troll.

'Simple,' said the Norn, smugly. 'They've tried telling him, like I said, and he isn't interested. But they know that Wotan doesn't know that the Ring-Bearer knows who Ortlinde really is. So they threaten to tell the Ring-Bearer, hoping that the threat will make Wotan tell Ortlinde to chuck it and come home.'

The troll stared at the bottom of his glass, trying to unravel the Norn's sentence. The Norn took this silence to mean that the troll was not yet convinced, and elaborated her point.

'You see, if Wotan doesn't know that the Ring-Bearer knows, then he'll be afraid in case the Girls tell the Ring-Bearer, and the Girls will try and get him to make some sort of a deal. The Girls can't make the Ring-Bearer chuck Ortlinde, because the Ring-Bearer presumably knows already – I mean he *must* know, mustn't he? But they can get Wotan to tell Ortlinde to chuck it if they can make him think that the Ring-Bearer doesn't know. Do you see what I mean?'

'Did you think all that up for yourself?' said the troll, full of admiration. The Norn blushed.

'That's very clever, that is,' said the troll. 'But what about the other thing?'

'What other thing?'

'You know.' The troll made a vague gesture with his huge paw. 'The other thing. I smelt it when the Girls walked in.'

It was the Norn's turn to look puzzled. The troll made a great effort and thought hard.

'Why was it,' he said at last, 'that old Wotan didn't turn the Girls into something when they gave him all that lip? You answer me that.'

'He tried to,' said the Norn. 'Just before he stomped off.'

'Exactly,' said the troll. 'He tried to, but he couldn't. There was something stopping him.'

'What?' cried the Norn, enthralled.

'I dunno, do I? But they brought it in with them. I smelt it. There was something looking after them, or at least it was looking after Miss Flosshilde. Didn't you smell it too?'

'I'm no good at smells,' confessed the Norn, who lived on a bleak, wet fell and had a permanent cold as a result. 'Was it some sort of Power, do you think?'

The troll had done enough thinking for one day. His mind was made of sandstone and, besides, he had other things on it. He looked at the Norn for a moment and for the first time in his life attempted a smile.

'You're very clever, you are,' he said. 'Do you come here often?'

The Norn blushed prettily. She noticed that the troll had very nice eyes, and if one of them happened to be in the middle of his forehead, who cared? The conversation veered away from the Ring-Bearer and the strange-smelling Power, which was ironic in a way; for the change of subject and the emotions that had prompted it were largely due to their influence.

The Norn had been right up to a point. Malcolm had discovered who the girl he loved really was, but not from the Rhinedaughters, or even Alberich, who had rushed back from Germany to tell him. He had heard and finally believed the news only when a sparrow had perched on his shoulder in Bond Street and chirped the information into his ear. By that time, of course, Malcolm was engaged to the girl, which made things all the more difficult . . .

It had only taken thirty-six hours for Malcolm and the girl who had come to catalogue his library to become engaged to be married. Malcolm was not quite sure why he had felt such an urgent need to get official recognition for this strange and unexpected outbreak of love in Middle Somerset. But it seemed the right thing to do, like getting a contract or a receipt. To his utter astonishment, his proposal had been accepted. The girl had simply looked at her shoes for a moment, smiled at him sadly, and said, 'If you're sure . . .' Malcolm had said that he was sure, and the girl had said something along the lines of Yes.

One is meant to do something wildly demonstrative on such occasions, but Malcolm felt too drained to waste energy in running about or shouting. In fact, he realised, he felt rather depressed, although he could not imagine why. For her part, the girl was even more taciturn than usual. The pretty scene had taken place beside the river in the grounds of the Hall, and they had sat in total silence for a while before getting to their feet and walking back to the house. At the door, the girl turned and looked at him for a moment, then muttered something about getting on with the catalogue.

'Catalogue?' Was she thinking about wedding presents already? 'What catalogue?'

'Of the library.'

'You don't want to bother with that, surely? I mean . . .'

'Oh, but I must.' The girl looked at him again, not as one would expect a girl to look at her future husband. Nor was it an 'Oh God what have I gone and done' look; just a look, that was all. Then she went up to the library.

Malcolm sat down on the stairs and put his hands over his ears. He felt confused, and no thoughts would come into his mind. With a tremendous effort, he called up the aspects of the situation that required his immediate atten- tion, and tried to review them in the detail that they seemed to warrant.

Unlikely as it seemed, he had just succeeded in getting himself organised for perhaps the first time in his life. He had fallen in love, and for a change the girl at the other end felt the same way. Instead of letting this chance slip through his fingers, he had got everything sorted out, and that was all there was to it. There was no earthly reason why he shouldn't get married; he had a house and money, which was what a married man was supposed to need, along with a wife. If there had been anything wrong with the idea, then the girl wouldn't have said Yes. She was obviously happy with the arrangement, and it went without saying that it was what he wanted most of all in the whole wide world. Was it? Yes, he concluded, it probably was. Mind you, it did seem a terribly grown-up thing to be doing, but then again, it would be, wouldn't it? So far as he could see, he was Happy. He lacked nothing, and had all sorts of nice things to look forward to.

Malcolm leaned forward, resting his elbows on his knees. It occurred to him that he had only known this girl for about a day and a half, and that he was being a bit hasty. He dismissed this thought, which was simply cowardice. The trouble was, he reckoned, he was probably afraid of being happy, of having what he really wanted. For some reason or other, which he could not be bothered to work out.

He got to his feet and walked slowly to the library. The girl was sitting at a table with a pile of books on it, writing something in what looked like a ledger. She did not hear him come in, and he stood looking at her for a moment. Life, he realised, was a fragile thing, and time and opportunity should not be wasted.

'Blow that,' he said, and the girl started. 'Let's go and buy a ring.'

His words had broken a deep silence, and silence followed them, so that Malcolm had the feeling that he was talking to himself. This would never do.

'Come on,' he pleaded. 'You don't have to do that now. Everything's going to be all right now.'

Oddly enough, the girl seemed to understand what he meant by that, which was more than he did himself. She smiled (why did she always smile and never laugh?) and said Yes, she would like that. So they went downstairs and Malcolm walked out to the garage to get the car.

Alberich was sitting on the bonnet, eating a ham roll.

'This is my lunch, you realise,' said the Nibelung. 'About the worst thing I could possibly have, barring lobster.'

'What are you doing here?' Malcolm asked.

'I came straight back from Germany,' continued Alberich. 'I saw the two of you together just now, and I knew in a minute what had happened.'

'Thank you.'

'You know who she is, don't you?'

Malcolm stared at him. 'Of course I do,' he said. 'Do you?'

'Well, of course.'

Malcolm frowned. How in God's name did Alberich know who she was? Did he have a library too? Malcolm suddenly felt that he didn't want to know.

'I know all about her,' he said. 'And we've just got engaged. We're going to London to buy a ring.'

'*Buy* a ring?' said Alberich, genuinely surprised. 'I'd have thought that was unnecessary.'

Malcolm did not understand this remark, so he assumed it must be a joke. Perhaps in the back of his mind he had an idea that Alberich was trying to tell him something very important, but if that was the case he managed to ignore it. He squeezed a polite laugh out of his lungs, and unlocked the car.

'Hang on, though,' said Alberich.

'Sorry, I haven't got time,' said Malcolm. 'I think we should get it in Bond Street. That's where all the jewellers' shops are, aren't they?'

'Why not Amsterdam? Or Johannesburg?' asked Alberich quietly.

'She wouldn't understand about the Tarnhelm,' Malcolm said. 'It might frighten her.'

'Most unlikely. Are you sure you know . . .?'

Malcolm started the engine and pressed the accelerator hard. Perhaps Alberich was saying something tremendously important; if he was, he couldn't hear a word of it. The Prince of the Nibelungs hopped off the bonnet and banged on the window. Malcolm wound it down and shouted, 'I'll see you when we get back. The housekeeper will make you a cup of tea, I expect.' Then he let in the clutch and drove furiously out of the garage.

Alberich stood for a moment and scratched his head. Then it occurred to him that he had been wasting his time. He picked up a spanner which was lying on the floor of the garage and hurled it at the wall.

Malcolm deliberately parked on a double yellow line in the middle of Bond Street. It was that sort of a day. If a traffic warden came and wrote him a ticket, he could tell her that he was engaged to be married to the most wonderful girl in the world. He wanted to tell people that, if only to hear himself say it. Anyway, he was feeling much better now, if a trifle hysterical.

The girl seemed to have cheered up, too. Almost for the first time since he had known her, she had laughed properly, and that was a wonderful sound to be anywhere near. In fact, Malcolm was at a loss to know what had got into her, for she behaved very childishly in all the jeweller's shops they went into. She insisted on trying on all the rings they saw, taking them to the window to see what they looked like in the light, and then saying that they wouldn't do. The stones were the wrong colour, or too small, or too big, or the settings were the wrong shape. It almost seemed as if she wasn't taking this business *seriously*.

They had tried six shops, and it was nearly half-past five.

'It's no good,' said the girl. 'I don't like any of the ones we've seen. And I'm the one who's going to be wearing it. For ever and ever,' she added, tenderly. For some reason, this remark struck Malcolm as being rather out of character, but he put it down to excitement.

'We can try that one over there, if we're quick,' he suggested.

'No,' said the girl, 'I know the ring I want.' And she told him. As she did so, it began to rain.

The two sparrows that had been eating crumbs outside the largest of the jeweller's shops looked at each other.

'Did you hear that?' said the first sparrow.

'Don't speak with your beak full,' said the other.

'But, Mum,' replied the first sparrow, 'it's him. And he's going to give her the Big Ring.'

'It's none of our business. And you'll catch your death if you don't get under cover this instant.'

'But, Mum,' insisted the first sparrow, 'if he gives her the Big Ring it'd be terrible, wouldn't it?'

'How many times must I tell you not to listen to what other people are saying? It's rude.' The second sparrow flapped her wings nervously. It was indeed terrible, and she didn't want to get involved.

'But do you think he knows how terrible it would be? Do you?'

'Quiet! People are staring.'

'It's rude to stare,' replied the first sparrow, who had been told this many times. 'If he doesn't know, shouldn't we tell him? Because if we don't . . .'

Two ravens had appeared in the sky, wheeling slowly and noiselessly above the street. Nobody noticed them; they had come to see, not to be seen.

'It isn't him at all,' said the second sparrow nervously, 'it's just your imagination. If you don't come in this minute, I'll tell your father.'

Malcolm was standing very still. The girl was smiling at him, saying nothing. He wanted to give her the Ring. He could see no reason why he should not. Almost from the first moment he had met her, he had wanted to give her the Ring, and now he was going to do it. It was the right thing to do. It was the only thing to do.

The young sparrow hopped morosely under a parked van. His mother was scolding him, but he wasn't listening. Surely it couldn't be right that the Ring-Bearer should give the Ring to Wotan's daughter. His mother stopped chirping at him for a moment, and stooped down to peck at a bottle-top. Now was his chance.

'Please,' said the girl. 'I'd like it very much.'

Malcolm took the Ring between the first and third fingers of his left hand and started to pull it off. He was afraid that it might not come away easily, but it slid off effortlessly, and he held it for a moment. The girl was still smiling, not holding out her hand, not making a movement of any sort. He tried to read her thoughts, but he could not. He could feel the rain running through his hair, but he did not know what it was. It was right that the girl should have the Ring. It would be very easy to give it to her. Nothing at all could

145

be easier, and then they would be properly engaged.

The sparrow forced itself through the air like a bullet and landed awkwardly on Malcolm's shoulder. He did not seem to notice. He had other things on his mind.

'Don't do it,' shrieked the bird. 'She's Wotan's *daughter*!'

For a moment, Malcolm did not know where the voice was coming from. Then he felt feathers brushing the side of his face, which made him jump. As he started, he dropped the Ring, which rolled into the gutter.

'She's Wotan's daughter. She's Wotan's daughter, she's his daughter!' screamed the sparrow. Malcolm swung his left hand furiously through the air and clapped the palm of it onto his right shoulder. He felt something fragile snapping under the fingers, and the voice stopped suddenly. The dead bird rolled down his arm and fell onto the pavement. It looked like a child's toy or a hockey-puck, and it had landed in a puddle.

Then the girl stooped down to pick up the Ring. Without knowing what he was doing, Malcolm covered it with his foot. It was all he was able to do, but apparently it was enough. The girl stepped backwards, and she had a look on her face that Malcolm did not like very much.

'I really do love you,' she said.

Without even wanting to, Malcolm found himself reading her thoughts.

'I love you too,' he said, and he bent down and picked up the Ring. 'If I offered this to you, would you take it?'

'Yes,' said the girl.

'And you'd give it to your father?'

'Yes.'

Malcolm closed his fist round the Ring. 'It's raining,' he said, 'you'll catch cold.'

The girl looked at her shoes and said nothing. He slowly put the Ring back on his finger. He wanted her to have it more than ever, but it felt terribly tight now, and he doubted whether he would be able to get it off again without soap and water. There was some quotation about there being a providence in the fall of a sparrow, but he had never really understood what that meant.

He opened the car door for her. 'Are we still engaged, then?' he asked.

'I don't know,' she said. 'Are we? I mean, is there any point?'

'But we love each other, don't we? Yes, we do,' he added, for he knew how indecisive she could be at times. 'And there's all the point in the world.'

'Everything I told you about my family is true,' she said, fastening her seat-belt. 'So I don't think there is any point, really, is there?'

Malcolm could not quite follow that one, but he wasn't bothered about it. He could read her thoughts. This was all so *silly*.

When they were on the motorway, Malcolm broke the silence that had lasted since they had left London.

'Obviously you know who I am,' he said. 'So you know I can read thoughts. I can read exactly what you're really thinking.'

The girl said nothing.

'Which is probably just as well,' said Malcolm irritably, 'since you never say anything. But I can see what you're thinking, so it's no use pretending. For crying out loud, you love me more than I love you.'

'That's for you to say.'

'Then be quiet and listen. You don't have to give him the Ring.'

'You don't have to keep it.'

Malcolm wanted to grab hold of her and shake her, but he was being overtaken by a lorry and needed both hands for the wheel. 'Don't you understand anything?' he shouted. The girl stared at the floor and said nothing.

'If I was feeling as bloody miserable as you are, I'd burst into tears,' he said savagely. 'But you won't let yourself do that, will you?'

He pulled over onto the hard shoulder and stopped the

147

car. Two ravens were circling overhead. Malcolm said a lot of things, some of them very loudly, some of them very quietly, and after a while he started to cry. But the girl said nothing, and there was no point saying any more.

'All right, then,' he whispered, 'you can have it. But not yet. Not yet.'

'I dunno,' said Thought, as he watched the car draw up at Combe Hall. 'Humans.'

The doors opened, and Malcolm and the Valkyrie Ortlinde climbed out.

'Now what?' whispered Memory.

Malcolm put his arm around the Valkyrie, and she rested her head against his face. The sharp eyes of the ravens could easily pick out the Ring, glittering on his finger. Neither the mortal nor the Valkyrie said a word as they went into the house, but the air was full of thoughts, and the ravens felt very frustrated that they could only read Ortlinde's half of them.

The door of the house closed and the two ravens sat thoughtfully for a while, listening to the wind sighing in the pine trees that surrounded the Hall. They had seen many things in their time. They had seen Alberich screaming with rage and pain when Loge tore the Ring from his chained hands. They had seen Hagen drive his spear between Siegfried's shoulders, and Hagen himself struggling for the last time in the floodwaters of the Rhine. Nothing surprised them any more.

'Thick as two short planks, both of them,' said Memory at last.

12

The girl – Malcolm could not bring himself to think of her as Ortlinde – was up at the crack of dawn cataloguing away like a small tornado. She at least had her work to occupy her mind; not that it was her proper work, of course.

Malcolm's own work was not going so well. According to the BBC, a rail disaster in Essex had been narrowly averted, and a nuclear reactor in Kent had been shut down in the nick of time, just before it had a chance to make the English Channel a little bit wider. Needless to say, these unhappy incidents had all taken place at the same time as he had been struggling to keep control of the Ring. It was an added complication, but no more. It wasn't that he couldn't care less; he cared desperately, but what could he do? He was the master of the world, but not of himself.

Alberich had been waiting for him when he returned from London. In fact, he had been pacing up and down in front of the garage all day, which had scarcely helped his digestion, with the result that he lost his temper when he caught sight of Ortlinde and called her some rather crude and unpleasant things. Malcolm had been on the point of hitting him again, but the dwarf had realised the danger he was in and apologised to the Valkyrie, blaming his bad manners on a cucumber sandwich he had been rash enough to eat while he was waiting. Now he had come back, and was sitting in the drawing-room, drinking milk.

'I know what you're going to say,' Malcolm said.

'Yes,' replied Alberich, 'you probably do. Whether you understand it or not is another matter. Giant's blood may have made you perceptive, but it hasn't stopped you being plain stupid.'

'Thank you,' replied Malcolm sullenly, 'but I can do without personal abuse.'

'Listen,' said the Nibelung. 'I told you before that you were too nice to be a proper Ring-Bearer. Ring-Bearers can't be like that. Sure, it worked well enough to start off with, but then it went all wrong. Well, didn't it? A nice but enamoured Ring-Bearer is capable of doing more damage in forty-eight hours than Ingolf managed in a thousand years. You're human; you can't help it. But you aren't qualified to hold the ring if you're human. Don't you see?'

'No.'

Alberich frowned. It was as if someone had said that they could not understand why rain makes you wet. It would take some explaining.

'Take my case,' he said. 'I'm not human, I'm delighted to say, but even so, the first thing I had to do before I was able to make the Ring in the first place was to forswear Love and all its tedious works. Whoever thought up that particular requirement knew what he was about, believe you me. Not that I was ever romantically inclined myself; my heart has often been burnt but never broken. Anyway, this made me immune from the one single greatest cause of idiocy in the world. Since I took the pledge, I have been smiled at by Rhinedaughters, yearned at by Valkyries, and generally assaulted by beautiful people of every species, all to no effect. And I don't even have the miserable thing any more. I'm just a peripheral character, especially now that you appear to have dismantled the curse I so cleverly put on the Ring. Or perhaps you haven't.' Alberich was thoughtful for a while. 'Perhaps this Ortlinde nonsense is the curse catching up with you as well. If it is, I'm sorry. Oddly enough, I don't feel any real animosity towards you, even if you are as stupid as they come. Curse or no curse, though, you've fallen head over heels into the oldest trap in the book. You really aren't fit to be allowed out on your own, let alone be the master of the universe.'

'I never asked for the job,' said Malcolm wretchedly.

'That's true, you didn't. But who cares? Shall I tell you about Love?'

'Must you?'

'Yes. The human race – we'll confine our attention to your mob to start with, although what I say is applicable to virtually all mammals – the human race has achieved so much more than any other species in the time it's been on this earth – a couple of million years, which is no time at all; about as long as it takes a sulphur-dwarf to learn to walk – that the imagination is unable to cope with all the things that the human being has done. The human race *created* Things. They built wonderful buildings, invented wonderful machines, brought into being poetry, music and art. To beguile their eighty-odd years they have every conceivable diversion, from the symphonies of Beethoven to the Rubik's Cube. They can rush round in sports cars, they can shoot elephants, they can travel around the world in days, or even hours. In virtually every respect, they have made themselves the equals of the Gods. Most of all, they have all the Things in the world at their disposal to use and entertain themselves with. And what do they like doing best of all? They like taking off all their clothes – clothes over which they have expended so much effort and ingenuity – and doing biologically necessary but profoundly undignified things to other human beings. Any pig or spider can do that, it's the easiest thing in the world. But you bloody humans, who can do so much that no other species could ever do, you can't do *that* efficiently. You agonise over it. You make an incredible fuss over it. You get it all wrong, you make each others' lives miserable, you write dreary letters and take overdoses. You even invent a medicine that deliberately makes the whole process futile. My God, what a species!'

The dwarf fell silent and drank some milk. Malcolm could think of no answer to the case as Alberich had presented it, although he felt sure that there was a flaw in it somewhere. Alberich wiped his moustache and continued.

'And so you give this irregularity in your minds a name of its own. You call it Love, which is meant to make everything all right. Rather than try and sort it out or find a vaccine, you go out of your way to glorify it. I mentioned your art and your poetry just now. What are your favourite themes? Love and War. The two things that any species can do, and which most species do so much more sensibly than you lot – screwing and killing – are the things you humans single out to make a song and dance about. Literally,' said Alberich, who above all else detested musicals. 'Now be fair,' he continued, 'can you honestly say that a member of a species with this ancestral fallibility should be allowed to rule the universe?'

'But isn't everybody the same? Don't the Gods and Goddesses ever fall in love? And didn't you once try and chat up the Rhinedaughters?'

Alberich winced. 'It is true that the High Gods do occasionally fall in love. You have, as a matter of fact, singled out the one race nuttier than your own. We Elementals have a far better record. The spirits of wood and stone have been known to make idiots of themselves, and I myself did go through a bad patch, I will confess. The spirits of wind and water – the Rhinedaughters, to take an excellent example – have so far proved entirely bullet-proof. But even when we do go haywire, we get over it very quickly and very easily. We see how stupid it is, and we pull ourselves together. Look at me. And your lesser Gods, your phenomena and abstractions and so on, have no trouble at all. Seriously, I should consider giving it best and handing the Ring on to a more suitable keeper.'

'Such as?'

'Modesty forbids.'

Malcolm shook his head sadly. 'It's not that I don't accept what you've told me,' he said. 'You've got a point, I'm sure. But I can't give you the Ring, much as I'd like to. I've promised to give it to her.'

'But surely . . .' Alberich rose to his feet, and then sat

down again, a hand pressed to his abdomen. 'Don't say I'm getting an ulcer,' he moaned, 'not on top of everything else.'

'You see,' Malcolm went on, 'the Ring isn't about all that any more. It's the only way I can prove to her that I really do love her. Don't you see how important that makes it?'

At times, Alberich said to himself, there are worse things even than dyspepsia. 'You haven't been listening,' he said.

'Yes, I have. But she's the most important thing in the world.'

'If you weren't bigger than me,' said Alberich, 'I'd break your silly neck. Make yourself shorter and say that again.'

Malcolm wanted to explain, but that would clearly be pointless. The Nibelung, he could see, had no soul. He offered his guest another glass of milk, but the offer was curtly refused, and Alberich left in a huff.

Having filled himself with the conviction that what he was doing was right, Malcolm went down to the library to seek confirmation.

'Hello,' said the girl.

'Hello, Ortlinde,' he replied. 'Funny, isn't it, the way all the people I talk to nowadays have German names?'

'You've got a German name.'

'No,' he said. 'My name's Malcolm.'

'They didn't tell me that,' said the girl. 'I think it's a nice name.'

'So is Ortlinde.'

'Thank you. It means Place of the Lime Tree.'

'I know.'

Malcolm remained standing where he was, feeling rather uncomfortable. The girl hadn't moved either, and Malcolm was put in mind of a boxing match he had once seen where both fighters had refused to leave their corners at the start of the first round.

'Are you really cataloguing the library?' he asked.

'Yes,' replied the girl, who sounded rather offended.

'Sorry. Did you really train as a librarian, then?'

153

'No,' said the girl, 'I never had an opportunity to have a career. But we've got millions of books at home, and my father never puts them back where he got them from. He's very untidy.'

'How old are you?' Malcolm asked suddenly.

'One thousand, two hundred and thirty-six.'

'I'm twenty-five,' said Malcolm, and he made some sort of a joke about having always preferred older women. Ortlinde smiled wanly.

'There's no point, is there?' she said.

'No point in what?'

'In going on like this,' she said. 'It's not your fault, really. It's my fault.'

She was looking down at her sensible shoes again; Malcolm wished that she might learn some sense from them. 'I lied to you,' she continued, 'I was sent to do something and I haven't even managed to do that. It's just that nobody's ever loved me before, and I haven't loved anyone before. But you'll be all right, I know you will. You'll meet someone else, and . . .'

'I don't want to meet anyone else,' Malcolm shouted. 'Ever again. I'm going to give you the Ring as soon as . . . as I've sorted everything out,' he finished lamely.

'But you can't. If you did, you would know I've let you down, and I would know that too, and you wouldn't be able to communicate with me and I wouldn't be able to communicate with you and this terrible resentment would build up and neither of us would be able to talk to each other . . .'

She talked, Malcolm thought, in the same way as a rabbit runs; terribly fast for a short burst, then a long, long pause, then another breathless sprint; and every few words, a little nervous smile that made him feel as if someone were crushing his heart like a cider-apple. Unless he found some way of cheering her up, life with her would be intolerable. On the other hand, life without her would be equally intolerable or even worse, so what could he do?

154

'Of course we'll be able to talk to each other,' he said firmly. 'All I have to do is give you the Ring, and I'll give it to you because I want to, because it'll show you that I love you more than anyone else or anything else in the whole world.'

'No, you don't. You can't. You mustn't.'

Malcolm felt as if someone had asked him his name and then contradicted him when he answered. 'Why not?' he asked.

'Because I'm not a nice person at all,' replied the girl, gazing tragically at her shoelaces. 'I'm nasty, really.'

'No, you're not.'

'Yes, I am.'

'No, you're not.'

She's probably never been to a pantomine, Malcolm reflected, so she wouldn't know. 'Really, you're a wonderful person, and I love you, and you love me, and it's all so bloody simple that any bloody fool could get it right. Don't you understand?'

Malcolm was shouting now, and the girl had gone all brittle, like a rose dipped in liquid oxygen. 'Come on,' he said, lowering his voice with an effort, 'we had it all sorted out a few hours ago. Don't you want to be happy?'

There was a long silence; not a pause for thought, but an unwillingness to communicate. It was like trying to argue with a small child.

'Well, don't you? Look at me when I'm shouting at you.'

'I don't know,' said the girl, looking even further away.

'Then . . .' Malcolm did not know what to say. Words were bouncing off her like bullets off a tank. 'Then you'll just have to trust me,' he said. He had no idea what that remark was supposed to mean, but it sounded marvellous. He put his arm nervously round her shoulder; there was no resistance, but it felt like touching a corpse, which was strange. Up to now, she had been the warmest person he had ever known.

He left the library and wandered out into the drive. A

155

small white Citroën was drawing up; it was the English Rose, back from her holiday. Malcolm groaned, and felt a totally unreasonable surge of resentment towards her. He knew that it had not really been his secretary who had invited the girl down to catalogue the library and so messed up his life. But on another level it had been, and that level suited Malcolm perfectly. He had found someone to blame for all his troubles.

'That bloody librarian you hired,' he started.

'Pardon me?' said the Rose. 'I engaged no librarian.'

'Yes, you bloody did. Linda Walker, Lime Place, Bristol.'

The Rose looked mystified. 'To catalogue the library? But Herr Finger, you refused categorically to permit me to arrange for any such operation to be performed. I obeyed your instructions on that point to the letter. The person you referred to is unknown to me.'

'Oh,' said Malcolm. 'Then I'm sorry.'

The Rose looked at him curiously through her spectacles.

'Is there a person of that name – Linda Walker of Lime Place – currently engaged in the work you described?' she asked.

'Yes.' Malcolm suddenly realised that he couldn't explain. 'Well, now she's here she'd better get on with it, I suppose.'

But the Rose seemed intrigued. 'Would she by any chance be a young person?'

'Yes, I think so.' One thousand, two hundred and thirty-six. Well, you're as young as you feel.

'Excuse me one moment.'

Before he could stop her, the Rose scuttled into the house. Malcolm followed, but his secretary proved surprisingly fleet of foot. She had reached the library door before Malcolm caught up with her, and she threw it open.

'For Chrissakes, Lindsy,' she wailed, 'what are you doing here?'

'Hello, Mother,' said the girl.

156

'Believe me,' said the Rose, 'it was none of my doing. I came here specifically to prevent any such occurrence.'

The three of them were assembled in the drawing-room: Malcolm slumped in an armchair, which threatened to swallow him whole, the Rose perched on the arm of the sofa, and the Valkyrie Ortlinde, the Chooser of the Slain, sitting on a straight-backed chair staring rigidly at a spot on the carpet. The English Rose had sent for tea; it had arrived, and was going cold.

'Who exactly are you, then?' Malcolm forced himself to ask.

'I am Erda,' said the Rose, 'also known as Mother Earth.'

'But you're American.'

'That is so; but only by adoption, so to speak. I went to the United States – long before there were any States, united or otherwise – to be as far away as possible from my ex-husband, the God Wotan. Since he refused to allow me access to my daughters, I could see no point in remaining in Europe.'

'You're Mother Earth,' Malcolm said dumbly. He wanted to argue this point. For a start, she was much too thin to be Mother Earth, but that line of argument would probably cause offence. He could see no reason to disbelieve the claim. Its very improbability made it plausible enough.

'And this,' continued the Goddess with a sigh, 'is my daughter Ortlinde. I need not ask what she is doing here.'

The girl said nothing, which was entirely as Malcolm had expected. 'Will someone please explain all this to me?' he asked pitifully. 'I'm only human, after all.'

'Certainly,' said Mother Earth. 'When I perceived that you had obtained the so-called Nibelung's Ring, I took it upon myself . . .'

'How did you find out?'

'I heard it from a nightingale who was present at the scene of the incident. I took it upon myself to place myself in a position where I could take an observer's role, and so

157

masqueraded as your secretary.'

'But they said you'd been here for years.'

'I am not without influence with the local minor deities,' said the Rose loftily. 'I am afraid you were misled.'

'You mean the auctioneer and the estate agent and all those people were gods of some sort?'

'Certainly not. Only the previous owner, Colonel Booth. He is the spirit of the small trout-stream that runs through the grounds of the house. It was through his co-operation that I was able to secure the use of this house, which I knew you had always wanted to live in.'

'And he's a god?'

'Only a very minor one. Many people are, you know; about one person in two thousand is a god or a spirit of some sort. Of course, most of these are mortal and wholly oblivious of their divine status. We prefer to keep it that way. It's like your English system of appointing laymen as Justices of the Peace.'

'And where's Colonel Booth living now?' Malcolm asked, expecting the man to appear from the stream at the bottom of the garden.

'I obtained a transfer for him to a tributary of the Indus. His family had served in India for generations, and he was most keen to keep up the tradition.'

Malcolm rubbed his forehead with the heel of his hand, but it did no good. The Rose continued.

'I assumed this watching brief with the express intention of making sure that my ex-husband did not try the so-called Brunnhilde option on you. In the past, as you are no doubt aware, it met with some degree of success in the case of your predecessor Siegfried, and I felt sure that if other options failed him Wotan would not hesitate to use it again. I had thought, however, that he had given up for the time being, and so took my annual holiday in Stroud.'

'Why Stroud?'

'I am very fond of Stroud. Apparently, as soon as my back was turned, Wotan implemented this strategy.' The

Rose paused, and looked sternly at her daughter. 'Perhaps you would care to leave us, Lindsy.' The girl got up and wandered sadly away.

'I must state,' continued the Rose, 'that I have only the best interests of the world at heart, and so my daughter's personal feelings must not influence my actions at all. Nor must they influence yours.'

'You're fired.'

'Mr Fisher, you do not seem to appreciate the gravity of the situation in which you find yourself. The situation as of now is extremely serious, and global security is at stake. To date, you have acted in a highly responsible manner towards the inhabitants of the world, and I felt confident that you could continue with this work without any undue interference from me.'

'Hold it,' said Malcolm. 'You arranged that damned gymkhana thing, didn't you?'

'Correct.'

'You must have known I'd have wanted to get my own back on Philip Wilcox. There was nearly an air disaster because of that.'

'It was a risk I had to take. Had you continued to remain enamoured of Elizabeth Ayres, serious repercussions would have ensued on an international scale. I had to ensure that such an occurrence would not take place. Similarly it is of the utmost importance that I dissuade you from continuing in a state of love with regard to my daughter Ortlinde. The love syndrome is a condition which no Ring-Bearer should be in for any prolonged period of time.'

'I know, I know,' Malcolm muttered. 'I've heard all that.'

'Then,' continued the Goddess, 'you will be aware that the termination of this unfortunate situation must be expedited. It is as simple as that, Mr Fisher.'

Malcolm laughed loudly for rather longer than the remark justified.

'Your natural reaction, I know, is to protest that the

matter is not in your control,' said the Rose. 'This is self-deception on your part.'

'Is it really?' Malcolm turned away and counted to ten. 'Why is it,' he said at last, 'that everyone I meet these days turns out to be a Goddess? You're a Goddess, she's a Goddess, the housekeeper is probably a Goddess.'

'Incorrect,' said the Rose.

'Oh, good. Look, I don't care, I just want to be left alone.'

The Rose continued with the same measured intonation, rather like the Speaking Clock. 'Correct me if I am mistaken, but you were primarily attracted to my daughter simply because you believed that she was not a Goddess but a normal, ordinary mortal. A somewhat counter-intuitive reaction for a human being, if I may say so; it seems to be a commonplace of human love that the lover believes his beloved to be in some way divine.'

This, Malcolm realised with a shudder, was the Rose's idea of a joke. After a pause for laughter, which was not rewarded by the expected reaction, she continued.

'Now that it transpires that she is not a mortal but merely a Goddess, your affection for her should logically cease. You may argue that she loves you . . .'

'You noticed that, did you?'

'Indeed. But her feelings towards you are simply the result of unclear thinking and underlying emotional problems, which I fear have now reached a point where the most competent analyst would be unable to help her. By extending reciprocal affection towards her, you will only cause her emotional situation to deteriorate; so, Mr Fisher, if I may be counter-factual for a moment, if you care about my daughter, you must stop loving her. It would likewise be in your own interest to desist, since you are doing considerable harm to your own emotional state which, I hardly need tell you, is by no means satisfactory.'

For the first time, Malcolm felt pity for Wotan. This sort of thing all day long would try the patience of any God.

'My husband was a similarly unbalanced person,' continued the Rose. 'His case should provide you with a most graphic illustration of the dangers of embarking on a serious relationship when the balance of the mind is, so to speak, disturbed. In short, Mr Fisher, it is imperative that you abandon your intention of giving the Ring to my daughter. You must set your personal feelings on one side entirely.'

'Get knotted,' said Malcolm violently. It was no way to talk to a Goddess, but he was past caring.

'Should you fail to do so, I regret to·have to inform you that you may well be directly responsible for global cataclysm. If my ex-husband were to resume control of the Ring, the consequences for the future of humanity would be at the very least severe, and quite probably grave. You yourself would undoubtedly fail to find the happiness you misguidedly believe would result from a relationship with my daughter; added to which, you would certainly be involved along with the rest of humanity in any potential Armageddon-type scenario that might arise as a result of my ex-husband's ownership of the Ring. In short . . .'

'Wrong,' said Malcolm. 'Wrong on every point.'

'Pardon me?'

'Where you go wrong is, you think that she'll give the Ring to her father. She won't. Never in a million years. You see, it'll be a present from me, the best present I could possibly give her. She'd never give it to Wotan or anyone else. She loves me, you see. In fact,' Malcolm said dreamily, 'she'll probably give it straight back again, and then everything will be all right.'

'I perceive,' said the Rose, rising to her feet, 'that I have been wasting my time with you, Mr Fisher. You have failed to grasp the significance of anything I have said to you. I can only implore you to reconsider your decision with the utmost diligence.'

'What do you actually do?' said Malcolm. 'What's your job?'

'Mostly,' said Mother Earth, 'I sleep. My sleep is

161

dreaming, my dreaming is thinking, my thinking is understanding. Consequently, my normal role is consultative, not executive. Only in exceptional circumstances, such as a threat of universal oblivion, do I undertake any active part in the day-to-day running of the world.'

'Yes, but what do you actually *do*?'

'I advise people,' said Mother Earth.

'Like the United Nations does, you mean?'

'There is, I suppose, a degree of similarity.'

'You're still fired. Now get out of my house.'

'Mr Fisher,' said the Rose, sitting down again, 'before I go and attempt to reason with my daughter, on the unlikely chance that she might listen to sense, let me explain to you the nature of what you call love. It is a purely functional system in the human operational matrix. With the lower animals, the urge to reproduce is a purely instinctive thing. The human race, being rational, requires a distinct motivation to reproduce. It has therefore been programmed to process the reproductive urge in a unique way.'

'Just out of interest,' said Malcolm, 'did you design the human race?'

'Correct. As I was saying . . .'

'Ten out of ten for the Ears and the Eyes,' said Malcolm, 'the Feet and the waste disposal system not so hot. Friday afternoon job, I always thought.'

'You are thinking of the hardware, Mr Fisher, which is the result of the evolutionary process, and for which I claim no credit or otherwise. My work was entirely concerned with the software, what you would call the feelings and the emotions. As I was saying, the human race needs a reason for everything it does, a reason it can understand within its own terms of reference. Love, companionship, sympathy, affection and understanding are simply the rewards that human beings must receive if they are to be motivated to do something that creatures of their intelligence and sophistication would normally regard as below their dignity. There are so many better things they could be doing. How long does a human being live, Mr Fisher? Between seventy and ninety years, given optimum conditions. Without some powerful motivating factor, they could not be expected to devote a major proportion of their extremely short lives to the creation and education of other human beings. Therefore, it was necessary to provide them with an incentive, one which they are programmed to accept as worthwhile. Love is nothing, Mr Fisher. You would do well to ignore it completely.'

With that, the English Rose departed, leaving Malcolm alone. His only reaction to these revelations, straight from the horse's mouth, was that it was a dirty trick to play on anybody. But the fact remained that he was human, and he was in love, and that nothing else mattered. If that made him a fool, then so be it; blame the person who invented the state in the first place. But he knew all about love; it was as real as anything else in the world and he could not deny its existence. He resolved to find Ortlinde and give her the Ring at once.

But she wasn't in the library, or anywhere in the house. Perhaps she had gone away. Perhaps her mother had sent her away, or taken her away by force. In his confusion, Malcolm did not use the Tarnhelm to take him to where she was; instead, he ran through the house and grounds calling out her name at the top of his voice. At last he saw someone sitting on the riverbank and ran across. The figure turned and, to his despair, Malcolm saw that it was only Flosshilde.

'Have you seen her?' he panted.

Flosshilde could not read people's thoughts like Malcolm could, but she could guess who he was asking after. 'Yes,' she said, 'I saw her just now down by the little wood, where you get that nice view over the valley. Not that she's looking at the view, she's sitting there looking at her feet again. Size six, at a guess. Mine are size four.'

'Thank you.' Malcolm turned to go, but the Rhinedaughter called after him.

'Well?' he said. 'What is it? I'm in a hurry.'

'I know,' said Flosshilde sadly. 'I've just got back from Valhalla. I was trying to get Wotan to send her away.'

'Not you as well.'

'It's for your own good.' Malcolm scowled at her, and she felt suddenly angry. 'Well, it is. But I failed. Wotan tried to turn me into a hedgehog and it was all for your sake.'

'A hedgehog? Why a hedgehog, particularly?'

'Fleas and things. But he didn't manage to do it for . . . for some reason or other.' Flosshilde had been wondering what had prevented Wotan from making that transformation. The one plausible theory she had come up with was what had given her hope.

'I'm sorry he failed,' Malcolm said, and started to walk away. Flosshilde waited till his back was turned, then deliberately pushed him into the river.

As he hit the water, Malcolm's mind was filled with images of the fate of Hagen, whom the Rhinedaughters drowned, and he instinctively turned himself into a rowing-boat. But the water was only two feet deep at that point, and after a moment he turned himself back again. For all her grief, Flosshilde could not help laughing.

'Shut up,' Malcolm snapped.

'I didn't mean it unkindly,' giggled Flosshilde. 'That was very resourceful of you.'

Malcolm had got his shoes and socks wet. He applied to the Tarnhelm for replacements. 'You just watch it in future,' he said sternly.

'You watch it,' said the Rhinedaughter. 'And look at me when I'm talking to you.'

It was true that Malcolm was looking at his shoes, but only to see what the Tarnhelm had provided him with. 'Have you been listening to us?' he said furiously. 'When we were talking just now?'

Flosshilde sat down on the bank and combed her long hair with an ivory comb that Eric Bloodaxe had given her many years ago. 'No,' she said, 'I've got better things to do with my time than listen to that sort of rubbish.'

Malcolm sat down beside her. 'Go on, then,' he said. 'I'm listening.'

'I went to see Wotan,' she said, putting the comb away. 'I tried to get him to call Ortlinde off. But he said he couldn't. I don't know if he was telling the truth or not, actually. Because if you go off with her, you'll be terribly unhappy, honestly you will. Even if it does work out, and you give her the Ring and she accepts it and all that . . .'

'How come everyone knows about that?' Malcolm said bitterly. 'You must have been listening.'

'It's the most important thing in the world right now,' said Flosshilde gravely. 'What do you expect? Like it or not, you're dealing with the Gods now. I know you don't like us very much, but we're important people. But never mind about the world and things like that. I couldn't care less about the silly old world, or the Ring, or anything. If you go off with her, you'll be utterly wretched. She'll make you miserable, I know she will.'

Flosshilde tried to open her mind to make it easier for him to read her thoughts, but apparently he wasn't interested.

'How the hell could you know?'

'Because you're not like that. You think you're in love with her, but you're not. You think that because she's in love with you, you've got to be in love with her. It doesn't work like that.'

'You're talking nonsense. It's not like that at all.'

'Shut up and listen, will you? You don't understand the meaning of the word Love. It's not that great big romantic thunderbolt you think it is. You saw her, you fell for her, your heart went mushy inside you. That's all totally silly; it doesn't happen that way. You don't know the first thing about her. How could you, you've hardly got two sentences out of her since you met. What are the two of you going to do for the rest of Time, sit around staring at your shoes, trying to make conversation? You both think you're in love, but you're deceiving yourselves. She thinks she's in love because she's always been treated like a piece of old cheese, and then you come along, looking like Siegfried himself, the most important man in the world, and start adoring her. And you fell in love with her because she's there and you thought she was a human being and so she counted. There's me, you thought; a real live girl, not a Goddess or a water-nymph, is actually in love with me. Whoopee, I'm not a failure or inadequate or as boring as hell, let's get married.'

'Have you finished?'

'No. You're stupid and silly and romantic, and you deserve to be miserable all your life. What sort of a world do you think you're living in? You're only fit to mix with Gods and fairies. You don't stand a chance in the real world.'

'Now have you finished?'

'You think you're strong and marvellous, don't you? But you're as blind as a bat and they're leading you by the nose. It's them, don't you see? It's Wotan's grand design, and you've fallen straight into the trap. I thought there was more to you than that, but I was wrong.'

Malcolm did not even bother to unravel this skein of metaphor. He stood up and walked away. When he was safely out of earshot, Flosshilde began to cry. As she sat weeping, her sisters put their heads above the water.

'You're just as bad as he is,' said Wellgunde.

'What sort of a world do you think you're living in?' sneered Woglinde. 'You're stupid and silly and romantic, and you deserve to be miserable all your life. Very well put, I thought.'

They laughed unkindly and swam away.

'Hello,' said Ortlinde.

'Hello,' said Malcolm. 'What are you doing here?'

'I wanted to be on my own,' she replied.

'I love you,' said Malcolm. He had grown used to saying that, and he no longer felt any embarrassment as the words passed his lips.

166

'You mustn't,' said the girl. 'Really, I'm not a nice person.'

'You said that before,' said Malcolm angrily. 'Don't try to be clever with me. I drank Giant's blood, remember? I can read what you're really feeling.'

'I've got no feelings, really. No emotions, no anything. Don't you see? I'm a Valkyrie, I'm Wotan's daughter. I can't be anything else, however hard I try. And if you try and make me be something I never can be, you'll only hurt yourself. I can't be hurt any more, I was born hurt. But I don't want to hurt you. So please leave me alone.'

Malcolm could not understand, but that was all right. He didn't want to understand and he didn't need to. He knew that she loved him, and this knowledge was like a gun in his pocket. So long as he was armed with it, no-one could touch him.

'If I give you the Ring, you'll take it?'

'Yes.'

'And you love me?'

'Yes.'

'What is so bloody fascinating about your bloody shoes? You love me?'

'Yes.'

'Oh, *good*. That's settled, then.' Malcolm shut his eyes and sat down, exhausted.

'No, it's not.' The tone of her voice had not altered, and she was still looking away. Malcolm could only feel frustration and anger, and he wanted to break something. The clouds grew dark, and there was a growl of distant thunder.

'You see?' said Ortlinde, sadly. 'That's why it wouldn't be any good.'

Malcolm could not understand this at first; then he understood. The storm was gathering fast, and rain was beginning to fall.

'Wotan never did it better himself,' she said.

'But I'm not like Wotan. He's a God and he's mad.'

'If only you'd seen my mother when she was younger,' went on Ortlinde. 'But they tell me I'm just like she was at my age.'

'One thousand two hundred and thirty-six?'

'More or less. That was before she left my father and went to America, of course. And my father was a nice person then, everyone said so. Do you know what he did to convince her that he loved her? My mother, I mean? You see, there was some sort of difficulty about them, just as there is about us. Anyway, to prove he really loved her, my father deliberately put out his left eye.'

'How could that possibly have helped?'

'I don't know, he never told me. We never talk about things like that. Besides, everything was different then, so it probably had some special significance. Anyway, that's how he got like he is now, that and marrying my mother. That's what love does to people like you and me and him, if we let it take over. The best thing to do with all feelings like that is to wait until they go away. They don't mean anything, you know. They hurt, but they're only feelings. They don't draw blood or make it difficult for you to breathe. They're all in the mind. Life is about eating and drinking and sleeping and breathing and working, and not being more unhappy than you absolutely have to.'

'For crying out loud,' said Malcolm. 'It's not like that.'

'What's it like, then?'

'I don't know, really.' Malcolm was unable to think for a moment. 'But isn't it just two people who love each other, and they get married and live happily ever after. I mean, so long as we love each other, what the hell else matters?'

Ortlinde made no reply. It was raining hard, but she didn't seem to mind. She was very, very beautiful, and Malcolm wanted to hold her in his arms, but on reflection he realised that that would not be a good idea. He called upon the Tarnhelm to provide him with a hat and a raincoat, and when they materialised he gave them to her, for he did not want her to catch cold. Then he walked away.

A pair of ducks had settled on the surface of the river, and as Malcolm walked back to the house they called out to him.

'Thanks for the weather,' they said.

'I'm sorry?'

'Nice weather for ducks,' explained one of them. 'Get it?'

'Very funny,' said Malcolm. He stopped and looked at the two birds, male and female. 'Excuse me,' he said.

'Yes?'

'Excuse me asking, but are you two married?'

'Well, we nest together,' said the female duck, 'and I lay his eggs. What about it?'

'Are you happy?' Malcolm asked.

'I dunno,' said the female duck. 'Are we?'

'I suppose so,' said the male duck. 'I never thought about it much.'

'Really?' said the female duck. 'I'll remember you said that.'

'You know what I mean,' said the male duck, pecking at its wing feathers. 'You don't go around saying "Am I happy?" all the time, unless you're human, of course. If you're a duck, you can be perfectly happy without asking yourself questions all the time. I think that's what makes us different from the humans, actually. We just get on with things.'

'But you do love each other?' Malcolm asked.

'Of course we do,' said the male duck. 'Don't we, pet?'

'Then how in God's name do you manage that? It's so difficult.'

'Difficult?' said the female duck, mystified. 'What's difficult about it?'

'So you love him, and he loves you, and you both just get on with it?'

'Do you mind?' said the male duck. 'That's a highly personal question.'

169

'I didn't mean *that*,' said Malcolm, 'I meant that because you love each other, it's all right. That's enough to make it all work out.'

'What's so unusual about that?'

'Everything,' said Malcolm. 'That's the way it seems, anyway.'

'Humans!' laughed the male duck. 'And it's the likes of you run the world. No wonder the rivers are full of cadmium.'

At the door of the house, Malcolm stopped. He did not want to go in there, and there was no reason why he should. After all, he had the Tarnhelm, so he could go where he liked. He also had the Ring, so he could do what he liked. This was not his home; it was only a tiny part of it. He owned the world, and everything in it, and it was high time he looked the place over. He closed his eyes and vanished from sight.

13

When sufficiently drunk, Loge will tell you the story of the
first theft of the Ring by himself and Wotan from Alberich.
According to him, when he realised that the Giants Fasolt
and Fafner were determined to exploit his clerical error to
the full and claim the Goddess Freia as their reward for
building the castle of Valhalla, he decided that the only
conceivable way out of his difficulties would be to find an
alternative reward which the Giants would prefer.

Finding an alternative to freehold possession of the most
definitively beautiful person in the universe, the Goddess
of Beauty herself, was no easy matter, and Loge searched
the world in vain for anyone or anything who could think of
one, starting with human beings, going on to the lower
animals, and finally, in desperation, trying the trees and
the rocks. The only creature, animate or inanimate, who
could think of anything remotely preferable to Freia was
the Nibelung Alberich, and when Loge asked him to
explain, Alberich rather foolishly told him about the Ring,
which first gave him the idea of stealing it.

Malcolm had heard this story from Flosshilde, who did
an excellent impression of Loge when drunk, and it was at
the back of his mind when he began his world tour. He
hoped very much that things had changed since the Dark
Ages. Certainly, some things were very different now;
Freia, for example, had long since fallen in love with a
wood-elf, with whom she later discovered that she had
nothing in common. Centuries of quiet desperation and
comfort eating had taken their toll, and Freia was no longer

the most beautiful person in the world. In addition, attitudes have altered significantly since the Dark Ages, with the discovery of such concepts as enlightenment, feminism and electricity; Malcolm hoped he would quickly find that he was in a minority in regarding Love as being the Sweetest Thing. A quick survey of the thoughts of the human race would, he felt, help put his troubles in perspective.

With magical speed he crossed the continents, and the further he went the more profoundly depressed he became. Admittedly, the concept of love took on some strange forms (especially in California), but by and large the human race was horribly consistent in its belief in its value.

No matter how confused, oppressed, famished or embattled they were, the inhabitants of the planet tended to regard it as being the most important thing they could think of, and even the most cynical of mortals preferred it to a visit to the dentist. Not that they were all equally prepared to admit it; but Malcolm was able to read thoughts, and could see what was often hidden from the bearers of those thoughts themselves. Furthermore, with very few exceptions, the human race seemed to find its favourite obsession infuriatingly and inexplicably difficult, and considered it to be the greatest single source of misery in existence.

Not that that was an unreasonable view these days. Human beings, as is well known, cannot be really happy unless they are thoroughly miserable, and as a result of Malcolm's work as Ring-Bearer, there was little else for them to be miserable about. Wherever he went, Malcolm saw ordered prosperity, fertility and abundance. Just the right amount of rain was falling at just the right time in exactly the right places, and at precisely the best moment armies of combine harvesters, supplied free to the less developed nations by their guiltily prosperous industrial brothers, rolled through wheat-fields and paddy-fields to scoop up the bounty of the black earth. Even the major armament manufacturers had given up their lawsuits against the United Nations (they had been suing that worthy institution in the American courts for restraint of trade, arguing that World Peace was a conspiracy to send them all out of business) and turned over their entire capacity to the production of agricultural machinery. The whole planet was happily, stupidly content and, in order to rectify this situation, mankind had fallen back on the one source of unhappiness that even the Ring could do very little about.

Despite this lemming-like rush into love, there was a curious sense of elation and optimism which Malcolm could not at first identify. He was sure that he had come across it somewhere before, many years ago, but he could not isolate it until he happened to pass a school breaking up for the holidays. He remembered the feeling of release and freedom, the knowledge that for the foreseeable future – three whole weeks, at least – all one's time would be one's own, with no homework to do and no teachers to hate and fear. It was as if the whole world had broken up for an indefinite summer, and everyone was going to Jersey this year, where there are donkeys you can ride along the beach. All this, Malcolm realised, was his doing, the fruit of his own innocuous nature. He remembered that when he was a child, a princess had chosen to get married on a Wednesday, and all the schools in the country had been emancipated for the day. It had been on Wednesdays that his scanty knowledge of mathematics came under severe scrutiny from a bald man with a filthy temper, and he would gladly have given his life for the marvellous lady who had spared him that ordeal for a whole week, allowing him to spend his least favourite day making a model of a jet bomber instead. Malcolm understood that he was now the author of the world's joy, just as the princess had been in his youth.

Actually seeing the results of his work made Malcolm feel unsteady, and at first he did not know what to make of it all. The world was happy, safe and in love, all except a certain

173

M. Fisher who controlled the whole thing, and a small number of supernatural entities, who were out to stop him. There seemed to be an indefinable connection between everyone else's happiness and his own misery, and he began to feel distinctly resentful. This resentment was foolish and wrong, but he could not help it. He had never wanted to take away the sins of the world. Once again, the old pattern was being fulfilled. Everyone else but him was having a thoroughly good time, and he wasn't allowed to join in. His subjects didn't deserve to be happy; what had they done, compared to him, to earn this golden age? Before he realised it, he was muttering something to himself about wiping the silly grins off their faces, and the clouds around the globe began to gather.

The first drop of rain hit the back of his hand as he sat in Central Park, watching the ludicrously happy New Yorkers gambolling by moonlight in what had recently been declared the Safest Place in the USA. A group of street musicians, dressed in frock-coats with their faces painted in black and white squares, were playing the Brandenburg concertos to an appreciative audience of young couples and unarmed policemen, and Malcolm began to feel that enough was enough. He wanted to see these idiots getting rained on, and his wish was granted. As the musicians dived for cover among the trees and rocky outcrops, a tiny Japanese gentleman saw that Malcolm was getting wet and ran across to him with an umbrella. Smiling, he pressed it into Malcolm's hand, said 'Present', and hurried away. Malcolm threw the umbrella from him in disgust.

He sat where he was for many hours, the rain running down his face, and tried to think, but he appeared to have lost the knack. For most of the time he was alone, and the only interruptions to his reverie came from the scores of ex-pushers who had moved out of cocaine into bagels when the bottom fell out of drugs. Just before dawn, however, a pigeon floated down out of a tree and sat beside him.

'Don't I know you from somewhere?' Malcolm asked the pigeon.

'Unlikely,' replied his companion. 'You were never in these parts before, right?'

'Right,' Malcolm said. 'Sorry.'

'That's okay. Have a nice day, now.'

The pigeon busied itself with bagel-crumbs, and Malcolm rubbed his eyes with his fingertips.

'The way I see it,' said the pigeon, 'you care about people, right? That's good. That's a very positive thing.'

'But where's the point?' Malcolm said, and reflected as he said it that he was starting to sound like the bloody girl now. 'I mean, look at me. I've never been so wretched in my whole life.'

'That's bad,' said the pigeon, sympathetically. 'By the way, are you British, by any chance?'

'Yes,' said Malcolm.

'They had a British week over at Bloomingdales. Scottish shortbread. You get some excellent crumbs off those things.'

Already the first joggers were pounding their way across the park, like ghosts caught up in some eternal recurrence of flight and pursuit. Two policemen, who had been discussing the relative merits of their personal diet programmes, paused and watched Malcolm as he chatted with the pigeon.

'There's a guy over there talking to the birds,' said one.

'So he's talking to the birds,' said the other. 'That's cool. I do it all the time.'

Malcolm looked round slowly. Only he knew how fragile all this was. The pigeon looked up from its crumbs.

'You seem depressed about something,' it said.

'I've got every right to be bloody depressed,' replied Malcolm petulantly. 'Everyone's happy except me.'

'My, we *are* flaky this morning,' said the pigeon. 'You should see someone about that, before it turns into a complex.'

'Oh, go away.'

'You're being very hostile,' said the pigeon. 'Hostility is a terrible thing. You should try and control it.'

175

'Yes, I suppose I should. Do you know who I am?'

The pigeon looked at him and then returned to his crumbs. 'Everybody is somebody,' it said. 'Don't feel bad about it.'

'I thought you birds knew everything,' Malcolm said.

'You can get out of touch very quickly,' said the pigeon. 'Have you been on TV or something?'

'How come,' asked Malcolm patiently, 'I can understand what you're saying?'

The pigeon acknowledged this. 'This makes you something special, I agree. But I'm terribly bad at names.'

'It doesn't matter, really.'

'I know who you are,' said the pigeon, suddenly. 'You're that Malcolm Fisher, aren't you? Pleased to meet you. Can you do something about this rain?'

Malcolm did something about the rain. It worked.

'And could you maybe make the evenings a tad longer?' continued the pigeon. 'This time of year, the people like to come out and sit by the lake and eat in the evenings, and this is good for crumbs. So if you put say an extra hour, hour and a half on the evenings, there wouldn't be that scramble about half-seven, with all the pigeons coming over from the east. It's getting so that you have to be very assertive to get any crumbs at all, and I don't think being assertive suits me.'

Malcolm promised to look into it. 'Anything else I can do?' he asked.

'No,' said the pigeon, 'that's fine. Well, be seeing you.'

It fluttered away, and Malcolm shut his eyes. He felt very tired and very lonely, and even the birds were no help any more.

At Combe Hall a small group had gathered in the drawing-room. It was many centuries since they had met like this, and they were very uncomfortable in each other's company, like estranged relatives who have met at a funeral.

Alberich broke the silence first. 'He has no right to go off like this,' he said. 'It's downright irresponsible.'

'Why shouldn't he go off if he chooses to?' replied Flosshilde angrily. 'He's been under a lot of pressure lately, poor man. And we all know whose fault that is.' She looked pointedly at the mother and daughter who were sitting on the sofa.

'Let's not get emotional here,' said Mother Earth. 'Unfortunately, we are all in his hands, and we can do nothing but wait until he sees fit to return.'

'I wasn't talking to you,' said Flosshilde. 'I was talking to her.'

Ortlinde said nothing, but simply sat and stared at the floor. Flosshilde seemed to find this profoundly irritating, and finally jumped up and put a cube of sugar down the Valkyrie's neck. Ortlinde hardly seemed to notice.

'That will do,' said Mother Earth firmly. 'Lindsy, perhaps it would be best if you went into the library.'

'Oh no you don't,' said Flosshilde. 'I want her here where I can see what she's doing.'

'This is what comes of involving a civilian,' said Alberich impatiently. 'Whose idea was it, anyway?'

'It certainly wasn't mine,' said Mother Earth. 'The first I knew about it was when I heard the reports.'

'That's what I can't understand,' said Alberich. 'Who is this Malcolm Fisher, anyway? Anyone less suited to being a Ring-Bearer . . .'

'But he's doing wonderfully,' said Flosshilde. 'Everything is absolutely marvellous, or at least it was until *she* showed up.'

'I'm not denying that,' said Alberich. 'But the fact remains that he's just not like any other Ring-Bearer there's ever been. Perhaps that's a good thing, I don't know. But if you girls had your way, he could easily turn out to be the worst Ring-Bearer in history.'

'Don't look at me,' said Flosshilde. 'I'm on his side.'

'Who chose him in the first place, that's what I want to know,' Alberich continued. 'That sort of thing doesn't just happen. I mean, look at the facts. He accidentally runs over a badger, who happens to be Ingolf. It doesn't make sense.'

'I confess to sharing your perplexity,' said Mother Earth. 'This is by no means what I had intended . . .' She stopped, conscious of having disclosed too much.

'Go on, then,' said Alberich. 'What was meant to happen?'

'I am not at liberty . . .'

'Since it didn't happen,' said Alberich, 'it can't be important.'

Mother Earth shrugged her bony shoulders. 'Very well, then,' she said. 'The Ring was supposed to pass to the last of the Volsungs.'

'There aren't any more Volsungs,' said Flosshilde.

'Incorrect. Siegfried and Gutrune did in fact produce a child, a daughter called Sieghilde.'

'I never knew that,' said Alberich.

'Nobody knew. I saw to that. Sieghilde was brought up at the court of King Etzel of Hungary, where she married a man called Unferth. A most unsuitable match, I may say, of which I did not approve. Unfortunately, I was too late to be able to prevent it.'

'And then what happened?'

'I have no idea. Unferth was an itinerant bard by profession, and I lost track of him in his wanderings. By birth he was a Jute, but he never returned to his native Jutland. I can only presume . . .'

Flosshilde ran out of the room.

'What's she up to now?' muttered Alberich. 'Why can't people sit still?'

'Anyway,' continued Mother Earth, 'given the quite remarkable fecundity of the Volsung race, I have little doubt that the family is still extant, and I have spent a great deal of time and effort in trying to trace the survivors of the line. Who could possibly make a better Ring-Bearer than the descendant of Siegfried the Dragon-Slayer? But to date my inquiries have been fruitless.'

'So you think there's a Volsung or two wandering about out there just waiting for a chance to snap up the Ring?' said Alberich. 'That's all we need.'

'On the contrary,' said Mother Earth, 'I still regard the Volsung option as being the best possible solution. The Fisher episode is surely nothing but a strange and unplanned complication which will undoubtedly resolve itself in time. As soon as the missing Volsung is traced and apprised of his destiny, we can all get back to normal.'

'That's not exactly fair on our young friend Malcolm Fisher,' said Alberich. 'He deserves more consideration than that. I presume that your Volsung would get hold of the Ring in the same way that his ancestor Siegfried obtained it from Fafner.'

'That ought not to be necessary,' said Mother Earth hurriedly. 'No, he has had his part to play as caretaker of the Ring, and to date I must grant you he has played it very creditably. Only this present difficulty has marred an unexpectedly satisfactory period in the Ring's history. Recent events, however, have highlighted the underlying weakness in his emotional composition which makes it obvious that he is not to be trusted with the Ring on a long-term basis. Unfortunately, as we have recently been made to realise, there is very little that any of us can actually do, when the chips are, so to speak, down, to influence matters. Thanks to Wotan, and of course to my daughter here, all may yet be lost.'

At this moment, Flosshilde came back into the room, carrying a volume of an Encyclopedia.

'Say what you like about old Misery-guts there,' she said, 'she's made a good job of that library. Here we are.'

She laid the book down on the table. 'The Jutes,' she said, 'were part of the Anglo-Saxon alliance that colonised Britain after the Romans went home.'

'I seem to remember hearing something about it at the

179

time,' said Alberich, 'now that you mention it. Go on.'

'If your Unferth was a Jute, perhaps he came over to Britain with the rest of them. Have you tried looking here?'

Mother Earth raised an eyebrow. 'I must confess that this is a line of inquiry that has not previously occurred to me. These islands have always been so unremarkable, heroically and theologically speaking, that I never for one moment imagined that the Volsung line might be found here. It is of course possible.'

Flosshilde seemed excited about something. 'Where would the records be?' she asked. 'This is worth following up.'

'The main archive is at Mimir's Well,' replied Mother Earth. 'I think it would be in order to check this new lead.'

'So what are we waiting for?'

'My dear young woman,' said Mother Earth, 'you don't expect me to abandon this highly delicate situation at this crucial juncture simply to go chasing through the files. It can certainly wait until Mr Fisher returns from his holiday and this present difficulty has been satisfactorily resolved.'

'Why are you so interested in tracking down this Volsung, anyway?' said Alberich suspiciously. 'I thought you were on Fisher's side.'

'Don't you see?' said Flosshilde. 'If we find the person who ought to have the Ring, Malcolm won't be able to give it to *her*, because it won't be his to give away to anyone. He's got wonderful principles, he'll see at once that he has to give it to this Volsung person, and then everything will be all right.'

Alberich shook his head. 'You overestimate him,' he said. 'Besides, what guarantee do we have that this Volsung will be any more suitable than Malcolm Fisher?'

'I can reassure you on that point,' said Mother Earth. 'I am, after all, the ancestress of the Volsung race. Admittedly, Wotan is their male ancestor, but that cannot be helped now.'

'You mean this Volsung would be her cousin?' Flosshilde asked, pointing rather rudely at Ortlinde.

'In strict form, yes.'

'Even so,' said Flosshilde, 'it's worth a try.'

'The Volsung race,' continued Mother Earth, 'was specifically designed from the outset to be Ring-Bearers. They have built into their software all the heroic qualities required to carry out that office in a satisfactory manner. Even after centuries of dilution, the fundamental ingredients ought still to be present. I have no doubts at all in my mind that if a Volsung or Volsungs can be found, our problems will be at an end. But first, it is essential that Mr Fisher's ridiculous idea of giving the Ring to my daughter . . .'

'Now there I agree with you,' said Flosshilde. 'Here, you. Haven't you got anything to say?'

'No,' mumbled Ortlinde.

For a moment, Flosshilde felt very sorry for the Valkyrie. Although she would have liked everything to have been Ortlinde's fault, it palpably wasn't, and the girl herself was probably having a rather horrid time. But Flosshilde hardened her heart.

'Why don't you do something useful for a change?' she said. 'You nip across to Mimir's Well and look up the records, if you're so good with libraries.'

Ortlinde shrugged her shoulders and started to get to her feet.

'Stay where you are,' commanded her mother. 'I'm not letting you out of my sight until this has been cleared up.'

Ortlinde sat down again.

'Well, someone's got to go,' said Flosshilde.

'You go, then,' said Alberich. 'You're only getting under our feet here, anyway.'

Flosshilde made a face at him. Mother Earth raised her hand for order.

'I shall telephone the Elder Norn,' she said. 'She is a most competent woman, and I'm sure Mr Fisher will not begrudge us the cost of the call.'

To telephone Valhalla from the Taunton area one has to go through the operator, and the process can take a long time. While Mother Earth was thus engaged, Alberich took Flosshilde on one side.

'You're up to something,' he said.

'No, I'm not.'

'Yes, you are. You're going to try and nobble this Volsung, aren't you? You failed to nobble Malcolm Fisher, so you want a chance at someone a bit more vulnerable, or at least with better taste.'

The Rhinedaughter shook her head sadly. 'My nobbling days are over,' she said. 'I've been nobbled myself.'

'Go on!' said Alberich incredulously. 'I thought it was all an act.'

'I wish it was,' sighed Flosshilde. 'But it isn't.'

'But what on earth do you see in him?'

'I don't know,' said Flosshilde. 'I suppose he's just different. He's sweet. I really have no idea. But I want to get him out of all this before they do something horrid to him.'

Alberich smiled. 'This is unusual for you, Flosshilde,' he said. 'I always thought you were the hardest of the three. Woglinde dries her face with emery paper and Wellgunde cleans her teeth with metal polish, but you were always the really tough cookie. And now look at you.'

'All good things must come to an end,' said Flosshilde, 'and I don't suppose he'll ever be interested in me even if he does get rid of her. Which is funny, really,' she said bitterly. 'After all, he's nothing special and I am, Heaven knows. But there you are.'

'There you are indeed,' said Alberich. 'Good luck, anyway.'

Mother Earth put down the receiver.

'Would you believe,' she said, 'the Elder Norn is away on her honeymoon. Apparently, she has married a rock-troll she met only recently at a Company meeting. But the Middle Norn has agreed to do the necessary work in the archives, so we can expect results shortly.'

'Well, that's something, anyway,' said Flosshilde, sitting down and putting her feet up. 'Now what shall we do?'

At that moment the door opened and Malcolm walked

in. His hair was wet, although it had not been raining in Somerset.

'They told me you were all in here,' he said.

'If you've got nothing better to do,' said the Valkyrie Grimgerde, 'you could fix that dripping tap in the kitchen.'

'I'm busy,' Wotan said angrily, but the Valkyrie had gone. He leaned back in his chair and poured himself another large schnapps. Despite the schnapps he was profoundly worried; it had been a long time since he had heard anything from Somerset, and surely his daughter should have succeeded in her mission by now. She was not, he was fully prepared to admit, an outstandingly intelligent girl, but intelligence was not really required, only beauty and a certain soppiness. Both of these qualities she had in abundance.

'Must you sit in here?' asked the Valkyrie Siegrune. 'I want to hoover this room.'

'Go and hoover somewhere else!' thundered the God of Battles. The Valkyrie swept out without a word, leaving Wotan to his thoughts and his schnapps. He bore the human no ill-will, he decided. His handling of the world, he was forced to admit, had been largely adequate. But this state of affairs could not be allowed to continue indefinitely, and if Operation Ortlinde failed, he could not see what else he could reasonably do.

'If that child messes this up,' he growled into his glass, 'I'll turn her into a bullfrog.' He closed his eye, and tried to get some sleep.

When he woke up, he saw that he was surrounded on all sides by daughters. Even allowing for his blurred senses, there seemed to be an awful lot of them. To be precise, eight . . .

'So you're back at last, are you?' he said. 'Well, where is it?'

All the Valkyries were silent, staring sullenly at their shoes, which were identical. When you have eight daughters, you can save a lot by buying in bulk.

'Where is it?' Wotan repeated. 'Come on, give it here.'

'I haven't got it,' Ortlinde said softly. 'He doesn't want me.'

'You stupid . . . what do you mean?'

He had spilt schnapps all over the covers of the chair, but none of his daughters said a word. This could only mean that Ortlinde had failed him, and they were all feeling terribly guilty.

'He wouldn't give it to me,' said Ortlinde sadly. 'He said that he loved me, but he couldn't give it to me. I knew it would happen, sooner or later. So I came home.'

'But why not?' screamed Wotan. 'You had the sucker in the palm of your hand and you let him get away.'

'I know,' said the girl. 'I've let you down again. I'm sorry.'

'Get out of my sight!' Wotan shouted. The girl bowed her head and wandered wretchedly away to clean the bathroom.

After a short battle with his temper, Wotan managed to control himself, and surveyed his seven other daughters with his one good eye.

'Right, then,' he said briskly, 'who's going to be next?'

There was a long silence. Nobody moved.

'Very well, then,' Wotan said. 'Grimgerde, go and do something useful for the first time in your life.'

Grimgerde shook her head. 'There's no point,' she said. 'He knows all about us.'

'He's been talking to Mother,' said Waltraute.

'He'd recognise me as soon as I walked through the door,' Grimgerde continued. 'It wouldn't work. I'm sorry.'

For a moment, Wotan was stunned. Then, with a roar like thunder, he leapt to his feet and ran out of the room. All the lights had gone out all over the house.

'We've let him down again,' said Grimgerde sadly.

'If only we could *talk* to him,' said Waltraute.

'Where's the point?' said Rossweise. 'We wouldn't be able to communicate with him.'

They went to fetch the Hoover.

14

Malcolm did not know where the others were, nor did he care much. He only knew that Ortlinde had gone. She had packed her suitcase, said goodbye, and walked down the drive, and for all Malcolm knew he would never see her again. Of course, he could not accept this; it seemed incredible that it could all be over, and at the back of his mind he felt sure that it was only a meaningless interruption to an inevitable happy ending. The girl loved him. He loved her. Surely that ought to be enough to be going on with. But she had gone away, and the part of his mind that still dealt with reality told him that it was for ever.

The room in which he had chosen to sit had not been used for many years; there were dust sheets over several pieces of furniture, and he tried to imagine what they looked like under their protective covers. There was half a tune he had heard in New York drumming away in his head; it was not a tune with any emotional or nostalgic significance, but it was there, like a fly trapped behind a windscreen, and he sat and listened to its endless repetitions for a while. In front of him were ten or fifteen sheets of paper on which he had started to write many drafts of the letter that would set everything straight. But the right words somehow eluded him, like a cat that refuses to come in when called. He could concentrate on nothing, and his eyes focused of their own accord on the walls and corners of the room.

'There you are,' said a girl's voice behind him. 'I've been looking for you everywhere.'

He knew even before he looked round that it was only Flosshilde. He said nothing. He did not resent her intrusion; nothing could matter less. He imagined that she would say something or other and then go away again.

Flosshilde sat in the window-seat and put her feet up on a chair. 'You don't mind me being here, do you?' she said.

'No,' he replied.

'I wanted to get away from the others. They were being awfully stuffy about something.'

Malcolm said nothing. He did not believe in the existence of anything outside this room, except of course for Ortlinde, and he wasn't allowed to think about her any more.

'Do you want to talk about it?' Flosshilde asked.

'No,' said Malcolm.

'I didn't think you would. She was rather beautiful, wasn't she?'

'She isn't dead, you know,' said Malcolm irritably. 'She still is rather beautiful for all I know.'

'What made you change your mind?'

'I had to do something. That seemed better than the other thing. I don't know. I did what I thought was for the best.'

'I think you were right, if that's any help. No, of course it isn't, I'm sorry. I'll be quiet now.'

'You can talk if you like,' Malcolm said. 'It wasn't bothering me.'

'Can you play pontoon?'

'No.'

'I'll teach you if you like.'

'No, thanks.'

'I know a game where you take a piece of writing – anything will do – and each letter has a number – A is one, B is two and so on – and you play odds against evens. Each sentence is a new game, and the side that wins gets five points for each sentence. Odds usually win, for some reason. That's what I do when I'm feeling unhappy. It takes your mind off things.'

Malcolm wasn't listening, and Flosshilde felt like a cast-away on a desert island who sees a ship sailing by without taking any notice of his signals. Perhaps it would be better, she thought, if she went away. But she stayed where she was.

'Shall I tell you the story about the time when the Giants stole Donner's hammer and he had to dress up in drag to get it back?'

'If you like.'

She told the story, doing all the voices and putting in some new bits she hadn't thought of before. It was a very funny story, but Malcolm simply sat and looked out of the window. Flosshilde wanted to cry, or at the very least hit him, but she simply sat there too.

'I want your advice,' she said.

'I don't think it would be worth much.'

'Never mind. One of my sisters is dotty about a man, and he's dotty about a girl, and she doesn't fancy him at all. What should she do?'

'Are you being funny?' Malcolm asked bitterly.

'No, really. What do you think she should do about it?'

'Grow up and get on with something useful.'

'I see. Aren't you sorry for her?'

'I suppose so. But I'm not really in the mood just now.'
He turned away and looked at the wall.

'I'm sorry,' said Flosshilde. 'I'll shut up now.'

She studied her fingernails, which were the best in the world. King Arthur had often complimented her on her fingernails.

'Would you like me to go and talk to her?' Flosshilde said after a long silence.

'Who?'

'Ortlinde, silly. Perhaps there's something I could say . . .'

'I thought you couldn't stand her. Why is that, by the way?'

'Oh, I don't know,' lied Flosshilde. 'We quarrelled about

187

something a long time ago.'

'Tell me about her. You probably know her a lot better than I do.'

'Not really,' Flosshilde said. 'I've known her on and off for years, of course, but only very generally. I find it pretty hard to tell those sisters apart, to be honest.'

'Are they all like her? Her sisters, I mean.'

'Very. Ortlinde's probably the nicest-looking, now that Brunnhilde's . . . And Grimgerde's quite pretty too, in a rather horrid sort of way. Big round eyes, like a cow.'

'I'm not really interested in her sisters. She said that the rest of them were all much nicer than she was, but I don't believe her. What did you quarrel about?'

'I honestly can't remember. It can't have been anything important. Is there anything at all I can do?'

'No,' said Malcolm. 'Perhaps you'd better go. I'm not in a very good mood, I'm afraid.'

Flosshilde took her feet daintily off the chair and walked out of the room. Once she had closed the door safely behind her, she shut her eyes and closed her hands tightly. It didn't help at all, and if she screamed somebody would hear her. She went downstairs.

From the landing, she could hear an excited buzz of voices in the drawing-room: Alberich and Erda and someone else, whose voice was vaguely familiar. The newcomer turned out to be the Middle Norn, a round, fair-haired woman in a smart brown tweed suit. She had brought a huge briefcase with her, and the floor was covered with photocopies of ancient parchments. Erda and the Norn were down on their knees going over them with magnifying-glasses, while Alberich was at the desk taking notes.

'. . . And she married Sintolt the Hegeling,' the Norn was saying, 'and *their* son was Eormanric . . .'

'What's going on?' Flosshilde asked.

'There has been a rather singular development,' said Erda, looking up from the papers on the floor. She had fluff from the carpet all over her jacket. 'We have succeeded in tracing the last of the Volsungs.'

'Really?' said Flosshilde. She wasn't in the least fascinated, for it scarcely seemed to matter now. Still, it would be something to do, and if she got bored she could play her word-game.

'I think you will be surprised when you hear it,' continued Mother Earth. 'Let me just go through the stemma for you.'

'Don't bother on my account,' said Flosshilde. 'I'll take your word for it.' She sat down and picked up a magazine. 'Just tell me the name.'

'There are three living descendants in the direct line,' said the Norn, taking off her spectacles. 'Mrs Eileen Fisher, of Sydney, Australia; her daughter Bridget, also of Sydney; and her son Malcolm, of Combe Hall, Somerset.'

In an instant, Flosshilde was kneeling beside them. She bullied the Norn into going over every link in the complex genealogical chain, which spanned over a thousand years. The descent was indeed direct, from Siegfried the Volsung, Fafner's Bane, to Bridget and Malcolm Fisher.

'I hurried over as soon as I found out,' said the Norn. 'Of course, you know what this means.'

'No,' admitted Flosshilde, breathlessly. 'Go on.'

'Well,' said the Norn, putting back her spectacles. 'Siegfried was, at least in theory, a subject of the Gibichung crown when he married Gutrune. Certainly, Sieghilde was a Gibichung subject, and so the Ring, if we accept that it was Siegfried's legitimate property, is subject to Gibichung law in matters of inheritance. Gibichung law is of course very complicated, and on the subject of testament it verges on the arcane, but it so happens that I have made a special study of the subject.' The Norn paused, as if expecting some words of praise. None were forthcoming. 'Anyway, hereditary as opposed to acquired property cannot, under Gibichung law, pass to the female heirs but is only transmitted through them to the next male heir. That is to say, to the female it is inalienable and she has no right to assign or dispose of it. She can only keep it in trust until the next male heir comes of age at fourteen years.'

'What are you going on about?' said Flosshilde.

'Although his mother is still alive and his sister is older than him, Malcolm Fisher is, according to Gibichung law, the rightful heir to the Nibelung's Ring.'

'Which ring?'

'My bloody ring,' said Alberich impatiently. 'Your ring. *The* Ring. Look, if we're going to be all legal about this . . .'

'Human law,' said Mother Earth loftily, 'has no bearing on property that is or has been owned or held by a God. Since the Volsung race is descended from Gods and is therefore semi-divine, and since the Ring was, if only for the space of a few hours, once held by the Gods Wotan and Loge, the Ring is subject only to divine law.'

'Oh,' said the Norn, clearly disappointed. 'Never mind, then.'

'Under divine law,' said Mother Earth, 'property descends by primogeniture alone. Mrs Eileen Fisher, Mr Fisher's mother – and the eldest surviving Volsung, is therefore the legitimate legal heir to the Nibelung's Ring.'

'What about me?' shouted Alberich.

'And me,' added Flosshilde. 'It was ours to begin with, remember.'

'The gold was,' said Alberich. 'But I *made* the bloody thing.'

'I was about to say,' said Mother Earth, severely, 'that under divine law, right of inheritance is subordinate to right of conquest.'

'What?' Flosshilde was now utterly confused.

'It means,' said Alberich bitterly, 'that if I take something away from you it becomes mine, and if they take something away from me it becomes theirs. That's divine law. Marvellous, isn't it?'

'In other words,' said the Norn triumphantly, 'it

amounts to the same thing as Gibichung law. It belongs to Mr Fisher.'

There was a baffled silence as the four immortals pondered the significance of all this.

'Be that as it may,' said Mother Earth at last, 'the fact remains that Malcolm Fisher, if not *the* last of the Volsungs, is one of the last of the Volsungs – certainly, he is the most recent of the Volsungs, which is roughly the same thing – and as such is by birth and genetic programming one of the three most suitable people in the world to be the Ring-Bearer. Goddammit,' she added.

Flosshilde could hardly contain her excitement. 'Just wait till I tell him,' she said. 'He'll be thrilled.'

'I hardly think it would be suitable at this juncture . . .'

Flosshilde made a rude face and left the room.

'That child is scarcely helping matters,' said Mother Earth.

'Guess what,' said Flosshilde, bursting into the room. 'You're a Volsung.'

'I'm sorry?' Malcolm said.

Flosshilde told him everything, putting in explanations where she felt they would be necessary. 'So you see,' she said, 'you're not really human at all. You're one of us. And *she* is your cousin.'

Malcolm laughed. 'What a coincidence,' he said sardonically.

'But don't you care?' said Flosshilde. 'You're virtually a God. You're descended from the world's greatest hero. Aren't you pleased?'

'No,' said Malcolm truthfully. 'I couldn't care less, to be honest with you. Of course, I always knew there was something wrong with me, but now that I know what it is, I don't see that it's going to make a great deal of difference.' He continued to stare out of the window.

'Oh, for pity's sake!' Flosshilde was angry now. She had so wanted him to be pleased and excited, and he wasn't. 'You're hopeless.'

'Very probably. And besides, from what you said, Bridget is the real Volsung, or the eldest, or whatever. That doesn't surprise me in the least. Judging by what I've heard about Siegfried lately, it sounds like she takes after him a whole lot.'

Flosshilde knelt down beside him and put her hands on his elbows. 'But she hasn't done what you've done. She hasn't made the world a wonderful place or defeated Wotan. You have, all on your own. You're the real hero, much more than Siegfried was, even.'

'Really?' Malcolm shook his head. 'I don't think so. I've stopped living in a make-believe world, you see. Just finding out that I'm a make-believe person doesn't make any difference. It's not going to change anything.'

'But you don't understand . . .'

'That's the one thing I have got right,' he said, looking straight at her. 'I *do* understand, and that's the only good thing that's come out of this whole rotten mess. I've been living in a world of my own and . . .'

'But the world *is* your own,' Flosshilde almost shouted. Suddenly Malcolm began to laugh, and Flosshilde lost all patience with him. As long as she lived, she told herself as she walked furiously out of the room, she would never understand humans.

On the landing she met the Norn, who seemed agitated.

'Call him,' she said. 'Something terrible is happening.'

Across the Glittering Plains, which stretch as far as the eye can see from the steep rock on which the castle of Valhalla is built, Wotan had mustered the Army of the Storm. In their squadrons and regiments were assembled the Light and Dark Elves, the spirits of the unquiet dead, the hosts of Hela. At the head of each regiment rode a Valkyrie, dressed in her terrifying armour, the very sight of which is enough to turn the wits of the most fearless of heroes. Around his shoulders, Wotan cast the Mantle of Terror, and on his head he fastened the helmet that the dwarves had made him from the fingernails of dead champions in the gloomy caverns of Nibelheim. He nodded his head, and Loge brought him the great spear Gungnir, the symbol and the source of all his power. When he had first come to rule the earth, he had cut its shaft from the branches of Yggdrasil, the great ash tree that stands between the worlds, causing the tree to wither and die and making inevitable the final downfall of the Gods. Onto this spearshaft, Loge had marked the runes of the Great Covenant between the God and his subjects.

Wotan raised his right hand, and the Valkyrie Waltraute, who closes the eyes of men slain in battle, led forward his eight-legged horse, the cloud-trampling Sleipnir. Above his head hovered two black ravens.

'If you get mud on that saddle,' said Waltraute, 'you can clean it off yourself.'

Without a word, Wotan vaulted onto the back of his charger. As the first bolt of lightning ripped the black clouds he brandished the great spear as a sign to his army, the *Wutende Heer*.

It was over a thousand years since the hosts of Valhalla had ridden to war on the wings of the storm, and the world had forgotten how to be afraid. Like a vast cloud of locusts or a shower of arrows they flew, blotting out the light from the earth. At the head of the wild procession galloped Wotan; behind him Donner, Tyr, Froh, Heimdall, Njord and Loge, who carried the banner of darkness. Close on their heels came the eight Valkyries: Grimgerde, Waltraute, Siegrune, Helmwige, Ortlinde, Schwertleite, Gerhilde and Rossweise, baying like wolves to spur on the grim company that followed them, the terrible spirits of fear and discord. Each of the eight companies bore its own hideous banner – Hunger, War, Disease, Intolerance, Ignorance, Greed, Hatred and Despair; these were the badges of Wotan's army. Behind the army like a pack of hounds intoxicated by the chase followed the wind and the rain, lashing indiscriminately at friend and foe. Below them, forests were flattened, towns and villages were swept away, even the mountains seemed to tremble and cower at the fury of their passing. With a rush, they swept over the Norn Fells and past the dead branches of the World Ash. As they passed it, lightning fell among its withered leaves, setting it alight. Soon the whole fell was burning, and the flames hissed and swayed at the foot of Valhalla Rock. As the army of the God of Battles passed between the worlds, the castle itself caught fire and began to burn furiously, lighting up the whole world with a bright red glow.

The army passed high over the frozen desert of the Arctic, convulsing the ice-covered waters with the shock of their motion, and flitted over Scandinavia like an enormous bird of prey, whose very shadow paralyses the helpless victim. As they wheeled and banked over Germany, the Rhine rose up as if to meet them, bursting its banks and flooding the flat plains between Essen and Nijmegen. Wotan, his whole form framed with the lightning, laughed when he saw it, and his laughter brought towers and cathedrals crashing to the ground. And as the army followed its dreadful course, black clouds of squeaking, gibbering spirits leapt up to swell its numbers, as all the dark, tormented forces of the earth were drawn as if by capillary action into the fold of the Lord of Tempests. The very noise of their wings was deafening, and when they swept low the earth split open, as if shrinking back in horror. But however vast and awesome this great force might seem, most terrible of all was Wotan, like a burning arrow at its head. As he flew headlong over the North Sea, the heat of his anger turned the waters to steam, and soon the forests of Scotland were blazing as brightly as Valhalla itself. As the army neared its goal, it seemed to concentrate into a cloud of tangible darkness, forcing its way through the air as it bore down like a meteor on one little village in the West of England.

'What's going on?' shouted Malcolm. The noise was unbearable, and through the splintered windows of the house a gale was blowing that nearly lifted him off his feet.

'It's Wotan,' yelled Alberich, his face white with fear. 'He's coming with all his army.'

'Is he indeed?' Malcolm replied. 'I want a word with him.'

All the lights had gone out, but the brilliance of the ball of fire that grew ever larger in the northern sky dazzled and stunned the watchers, so that even Mother Earth had to turn away. But Malcolm walked calmly out of the shattered door and stood in the drive. His hair was unruffled and his eyes were unblinking, and on his finger the Ring felt easy and comfortable. Out of the immeasurable darkness that surrounded it the awful light grew ever more fierce, until the very ground seemed to be about to melt. Like a falling sun, it hurtled towards the ruined house, straight at the Ring-Bearer, like a diving falcon.

'All right,' said Malcolm sternly. 'That will do.'

The light went out, and the world was plunged into utter darkness. A hideous scream cut through the air like a spearblade through flesh, and was held for an instant in the hollow of the surrounding hills. Then it died away, and the cloud slowly began to fall apart. Like a swarm of angry bees suddenly confounded by a puff of smoke, Wotan's army sank out of the air and disintegrated. The black vapours dissolved, and the gentle light of the sun fell upon the surfaces of the wrecked and mangled planet.

'And before you go,' said Malcolm, 'you can clear up all this mess.'

Like a film being wound back, the world began to reassemble itself. Smoke was dragged out of the air back into the stumps of charred trees. Bricks and stones slipped back into place and once more were houses. Glass re-formed itself smoothly into panes, and the cracks faded away. The flooded rivers slid shamefacedly back between their banks, taking their silt with them, and the earth silently closed up its fissures. While this remarkable act of healing was taking place, a pale mist formed and hung in the still air above the surface of the world, and the light of the sun was caught and refracted by it into all the colours of the spectrum. Malcolm had never seen anything so beautiful in his entire life.

'What is it?' he asked a passing dove. The bird looked puzzled for a moment.

'Oh, *that*,' it said at last. 'That's just the Test Card.'

Malcolm shrugged his shoulders and walked back into the house.

The drawing-room seemed to be deserted, and Malcolm had come to the conclusion that everyone must have got bored and gone away when he heard a voice from under the table.

'What happened?' said the voice.

'Nothing,' said Malcolm. 'It's over now.'

Looking rather ashamed of herself, Mother Earth crawled out from her hiding-place. 'I dropped my god-damned glasses,' she mumbled. 'I was just looking for them, and . . .'

'Are you sure they're not in your pocket?' asked Malcolm sympathetically. Mother Earth made a dumb show of looking in her pocket and, not surprisingly, there they were. 'Thank you,' she said humbly.

'You're welcome,' said Malcolm.

Alberich and the Middle Norn emerged from behind the sofa. To his amusement, Malcolm saw that Alberich was holding the Norn's hand in a comforting manner.

'There now,' said the dwarf, 'I told you it would be all right, didn't I?'

The Norn beamed at him, her round face illuminated by some warm emotion. 'I don't know what came over me,' she said.

'That was very clever,' Alberich said to Malcolm, forgetting to let go of the Norn's hand even though the danger was past. 'How did you manage it?'

'What, that?' said Malcolm diffidently. 'Oh, it was nothing, really.'

Alberich and his new friend walked to the window. In the sky there was a deep red glow, which could have been the sunset were it not for the fact that it was due North. Alberich looked at it for a long time.

'I never did like them,' he said at last.

'Who?' Malcolm asked.

'The Gods,' said Alberich. Then he turned to the Norn. 'You look like you could do with some fresh air,' he said. 'Do you fancy a stroll in the garden?'

It seemed very probable that she did, and they walked away arm in arm. Malcolm shook his head sadly.

'Who was that, by the way?' he asked Mother Earth, who was busily brushing the fluff off her jacket.

'The Middle Norn,' said Mother Earth.

'Doesn't she have a name?'

'I don't know. Probably.'

'What's that light in the sky? I thought I'd put everything right.'

'That is the castle of Valhalla in flames,' replied Mother Earth quietly. 'The High Gods have all gone down. They no longer exist.'

Malcolm stared at her for a moment. 'All of them?'

'All of them. Wotan, Donner, Tyr, Froh . . .'

'*All* of them?'

'They went against the power of the Ring,' said Mother Earth with a shrug, 'and were proved to be weaker.'

'And what about the Valkyries?' Malcolm's throat was suddenly dry.

'They were only manifestations of Wotan's mind,' said Mother Earth. 'Figments of his imagination, I suppose you could say.'

'But they were your daughters.'

'In a sense.' Mother Earth polished her spectacles and

put them precisely on her nose. 'But what the hell, I never really got on with them. Not as *people*. They were too like their father, I guess, and boy, am I glad to see the back of him.'

'And they're all dead?'

'Not dead,' said Mother Earth firmly. 'They just don't exist any more. I wouldn't upset yourself over it. In fact, you should be pretty pleased with yourself. By the way, did Flosshilde tell you about . . .?'

'Yes,' said Malcolm, 'yes, she did.' He was trying to remember what Ortlinde had looked like, but strangely enough he couldn't. He felt as if he had been woken up in the middle of a strange and wonderful dream, and that all the immensely real images that had filled his mind only a moment ago were slipping away from him, like water that you try and hold in your hand.

'Let me assure you,' said Mother Earth, 'that you have in no sense *killed* anybody.'

'I don't believe I have,' said Malcolm slowly, 'I think I'm beginning to understand all this business after all. By the way, what happens now?'

Mother Earth came as close as she had ever done to a smile. 'You tell me,' she said. 'You're in charge now.'

Malcolm looked at the Ring on his finger. 'Right,' he said, 'let's get this show on the road.'

Mother Earth yawned. 'I'm feeling awful sleepy,' she said. 'I guess I'll go to bed now, if you don't mind. If I don't get my thousand years every age I'm no use to anybody.'

'Go ahead,' said Malcolm. 'And thanks for all your help.'

'You're welcome,' said Mother Earth. She was beginning to glow with a pale blue light. 'I didn't do anything, really. It was all your work.'

Malcolm smiled, and nodded.

'Remember,' she said, 'whatever you feel like doing is probably right.' She was indistinct now, and Malcolm could see a coffee-table through her.

198

'Sorry?' he asked, but she had melted away, leaving only a few sparkles behind her in the air. Malcolm shrugged his shoulders.

'Never mind,' he said aloud. 'She's probably on the phone.'

Two very bedraggled ravens floated down out of the evening sky and pecked at the window-pane. Their feathers were slightly singed. Malcolm opened the window and they hopped painfully into the room.

'Hello,' said Malcolm. 'What can I do for you?'

The first raven nudged his companion, who nudged him back.

'We were thinking,' said the first raven. 'You might be wanting a messenger service.'

'Now you've taken over,' said the second raven.

'You see,' said the first raven, 'we used to work for the old management, and now they've been wound up . . .'

'What do you do, exactly?' Malcolm asked.

'We fly around the world and see what's going on,' said the raven, 'and then we come and tell you.'

'That sounds fine,' said Malcolm. 'You're on.'

The second raven dipped its beak gratefully. 'I was thinking of packing it in,' he said. 'But now the old boss has gone . . .'

'What are you called?' Malcolm asked.

'I'm Thought,' said the first raven, 'and this is Memory.'

'When can you start?'

Thought seemed to hesitate, but Memory said, 'Straight away.' When Malcolm wasn't looking, Thought pecked his colleague hard on the shoulder.

'Fine,' said Malcolm. 'First, go and make sure that all the damage has been put right. Then check to see if any of the old Gods are still left over.'

The two ravens nodded and fluttered away. When they were (as they thought) out of earshot, Thought turned to Memory and said, 'What did you tell him that for?'

'What?' said Memory.

199

'About us starting straight away. I wanted a holiday.'

'Don't you ever think?' replied Memory. 'This is the twentieth century. They've got telephones, they've got computers, they've got Fax machines. They don't need birds any more. Nobody's indispensable, chum. You've got to show you're willing to work.'

'Oh, well,' said Thought. 'Here we go again, then.'

After a while, it occurred to Malcolm that he hadn't seen Flosshilde since the storm had died away. At the back of his mind something told him that now that Ortlinde no longer existed, it was time to move on to the next available option, but he recognised that instinct and deliberately cut it out of his mind. It was the old Malcolm Fisher instinct, the one that made him fall in love and be unhappy. He was finished with all that now. He knew of course that there was such a thing as love, and that if you happen to come across it, as most people seem to do, it is not a thing that you can avoid, or that you should want to avoid. But you cannot go out and find it, because it is not that sort of creature. The phrase 'to fall in love', he realised, is a singularly apt one; it is something you blunder into, like a pothole. Very like a pothole. In his case, however, he had had the fortune, good or bad, to blunder into a badger, not love, and since he was not accident-prone, that was probably all the accidental good fortune he was likely to get. As for Flosshilde – well, since the passing of the Valkyries, she was officially one of the three prettiest girls in the universe, but only superficial people judge by appearances. Malcolm himself could be a prettier girl than Flosshilde just by giving an order to the Tarnhelm, although it was unlikely that he should ever want to do that. The fact that she was a water-spirit was neither here nor there; he himself was a hero, descended from Mother Earth and a now non-existent God, but he doubted whether that had any influence on his character or behaviour. He suddenly realised that Wotan and Erda and

200

all the rest of them had been his relatives. That at least explained why he had been frightened of them and why he had found them so difficult to cope with.

He smiled at this thought. Family is family, after all, and he had just blotted most of his out. But now he was on his own, which, bearing in mind the case of his unhappy predecessor, was probably no bad thing. It would be foolish to go looking for a consort now that the world depended on him and him alone. A trouble shared, after all, is a trouble doubled.

Nevertheless, he wondered where Flosshilde had got to. Everyone seemed to have drifted away, and for a moment he felt a slight panic. He sat down on the stairs and tried to think calmly. To his relief, he found this perfectly possible to do.

Wotan, he reflected, had gone to one extreme, but Ingolf had gone to the other. One had been caught up in a noisy and infuriating household which had driven him quietly mad. The other had curled up in a hole and allowed his dark subconscious to permit the world to drift into the twentieth century, with all its unpleasant consequences. He sought a happy medium between these two extremes, and in particular considered carefully all that Mother Earth had told him. Then he got up and whistled loudly. To his surprise, nothing happened. Then he realised his mistake and went through to the drawing-room. There were the two ravens, huddled upon the window-sill.

'Everything's fine,' said Thought, as soon as Malcolm had let them in. 'All the Gods have cleared off.'

'Except Loge,' said Memory. 'He offered us all the dead sheep we could eat if we didn't tell you he was still around, but we thought . . .'

'I've got nothing against Loge,' said Malcolm. 'But how come he didn't go down with all the others?'

'He was a bit puzzled by that,' said Memory. 'Apparently, there he was, surrounded by Gods one minute, all on his own feeling a right prat the next. He thinks it's down to him being a fire-spirit and not a real God.'

'Tell him he can have his old job back if he wants it,' said Malcolm.

'I'll tell him,' said Thought, 'but I think he's got other plans. He was talking about going into the wet fish business. Muttered something about he might as well do it himself before somebody did it to him. Gloomy bloke, I always thought.'

'Anyway,' said Malcolm, 'did either of you see Flosshilde?'

'Flosshilde,' said Memory thoughtfully. 'Can't say I did. In fact, I haven't seen any of the girls since before the Big Bang.'

Malcolm suddenly felt very ill. 'But they weren't High Gods, were they?' he said. 'I mean, they couldn't have . . .'

'Wouldn't have thought so,' said Memory, 'but you never know with those three. Very deep they were, though you wouldn't think it to look at them. But they were always mixed up with some pretty heavy things, like the Rhinegold and the Ring. Could be that they had to go along with the rest.'

Malcolm sat down heavily, appalled at the thought. He couldn't understand why he was so horrified, but the idea of never seeing Flosshilde again suddenly seemed very terrible. Not that he was in love with her; but he knew now that he needed her very urgently.

'Find her,' he snapped. 'Go on, move. If you're not back by dawn. I'll turn you both into clay pigeons.'

The ravens flapped hurriedly away into the night, and Malcolm closed his eyes and groaned. He had just bumped into something, and it felt horribly disconcerting.

'Oh, God,' he said aloud. 'Now look what I've done.'

Alberich and the Middle Norn looked in to say goodbye, and found Malcolm in a strange mood. He seemed upset about something but would not say what it was, and his manner seemed cold and hostile. The Norn felt sorry for him, but Alberich seemed in a hurry to get away.

'I don't like it,' he said. 'Something's gone wrong.'

'What could possibly go wrong now?' said the Norn coyly.

'I don't know,' said Alberich, 'but when it does, I want to be safely underground, where it won't matter so much.'

They walked in silence for a while, as the Norn nerved herself to ask the question that had been worrying her.

'Alberich,' she said.

'Yes?'

'Don't take this the wrong way, but weren't you supposed to have foresworn Love?'

'Yes,' said Alberich, 'but I'm allowed to change my mind, aren't I?'

'But I didn't think you could. Not once you'd sworn.'

'That was conditional on my still wanting the Ring. And now that I couldn't care less about it . . .'

'Couldn't you?'

'No.' He felt rather foolish, but for some reason that was all that seemed to be wrong with him. An unwonted harmony seemed to have overtaken his digestive system.

'To celebrate,' he said daringly, 'let's go and treat ourselves to the best lunch money can buy in this godforsaken country. I've heard about this place where you can get very palatable lobster.'

The Norn stared at him. 'Are you sure?' she said.

Alberich smiled at her fondly. 'Don't you start,' he said.

It was nearly dawn by the time the ravens came back. They perched on the window-sill exhausted, for they had been flying hard all night. Through the open window, they could see the new Lord of Tempests sitting where he had been when they had left him several hours before. He was staring at the ground, and he looked distinctly irritable.

'He's not going to like it,' whispered Memory.

'You tell him,' replied Thought. 'You're the one with the words.'

'Why's it always got to be me?' said Memory angrily. 'You're the eldest, you tell him.'

'How do you make that out?'

'Stands to reason, dunnit? You can't have memory before thought, or you wouldn't have anything to remember. Well, would you?'

Memory clearly had right on his side, and so it was Thought who tapped gingerly on the pane and hopped into the room first. Malcolm looked up, and there was something in his eyes that both ravens recognised.

'Well?'

'Nothing, boss,' said Thought. 'We did all the rivers, oceans, seas, lakes, lochs, lagoons, burns and wadis in the world. Even did the reservoirs and the sewers. Nothing. Looks like they've just . . .'

Malcolm let out a long, low moan, and Thought stepped back nervously, expecting every moment to be turned into a small flat disc made of pitch, earmarked for certain destruction. But Malcolm simply nodded, and the two birds flew thankfully away.

'Now look what you've gone and done,' said Thought bitterly as they collapsed onto a fallen tree beside the trout-stream. 'You've gone and got us saddled with another bloody nutter. The last one was bad enough . . .'

'How was I to know he'd go off his rocker?' said Memory. 'He looked all right to me.'

'You never learn, do you?' continued Thought. 'We could be well away by now, but no, you've got to go and *volunteer* us. If we ever get out of this in one piece . . .'

In view of the threat recently uttered by the new Lord of the Ravens, that seemed improbable. Dawn was breaking in the East, and Thought regarded it sourly.

'Look at that,' he said. 'No imagination, this new bloke.'

'Come on,' said Memory. 'We might as well have another go.'

They lifted themselves wearily into a thermal and floated away.

204

15

For about a week after the going-down of the old Gods, Malcolm was kept rather busy. Minor spirits and divine functionaries called at all hours of the day and night with papers for him to read and documents to sign, most of which were concerned with trivial matters. The remaining Gods had been stripped of the last few vestiges of authority by the destruction of Wotan and, try as they might, they could not persuade the Ring-Bearer to transfer any of his duties or powers to them. In the end the majority of them accepted the new order of things, and the few recalcitrant deities who continued to protest found themselves posted to remote and uninhabited regions where their ineffectual energies could be expended without causing any real disturbance.

In an effort to appear positive, Malcolm created a new class of tutelary deities. The rivers and oceans had long had their own guardian spirits, originally installed when shipping was the main form of transport in the world. In the last few centuries, however, this role had diminished, whereas the roads and railways had gone without any form of heavenly representation. Malcolm therefore assigned most of the redundant spirits to the railway networks and motorways, a system which seemed to satisfy most requirements. He commissioned the Norns to set up a system of appointments: all gods wishing to be assigned a road or a railway had to take a written exam, and were posted according to the results they obtained. Since their duties were strictly honorary, it made little difference to the world at la.ᵉ, but it seemed to please the divine community. It gave them a purpose in life, and when one is dealing with immortals, that is no mean achievement.

There were also vacancies in existing posts to be filled, for many river-spirits and cloud-shepherds had perished with their master in the attack on Combe Hall. Again, the Norns were given the task of drawing up a list of unfilled posts, with a parallel list of suitable candidates. Malcolm, who was unfamiliar with divine prosopography, had to rely heavily on the judgement of his advisers, but for some reason virtually all the supernatural beings he met were patently terrified of him, and this terror, combined with his ability to read thoughts, made corruption or favouritism seem unlikely.

He found the terror he inspired in his subordinates extremely hard to understand. Admittedly, his patience was sorely tried at times, for all the gods and spirits took themselves extremely seriously even though their power was non-existent; and he had to admit that he did sometimes lose his temper with them, causing the occasional shower of unplanned rain. But the world continued to thrive and prosper, with only the epidemic of love and romance spoiling an otherwise perfect situation. One thing did worry him, however: the Tarnhelm seemed to have developed a slight fault. Occasionally, after a particularly trying meeting or a long night of paperwork, he found to his disgust that he had changed his shape without wanting to, and for some reason the shape the Tarnhelm selected for him was invariably that of Wotan. This and a curious craving for schnapps gave Malcolm pause for thought, but he dismissed his fears as paranoia, and carried on with the work of reorganisation.

But he was not happy. Although he could not remember what she had looked like, he knew that Ortlinde was very much on his mind, and he could not help feeling horribly guilty about having caused her to cease to exist. He closed up the library at Combe Hall, but the house itself seemed to be haunted by her, and eventually he decided that the time had come to leave it for good. He sent for Colonel Booth (whose real name, he discovered, was Guttorm), thanked him for the loan of his house, and started to look for a new place to live. Somehow, he felt no enthusiasm for the task, and although the Norns, whom he found invaluable, continually sent him details of highly attractive properties all over the world, he found it difficult to summon up the energy to go and view them. Then one day the Younger Norn remarked that there was always Valhalla itself . . .

'But I thought it had been burnt down,' Malcolm said.

'Burnt, yes,' said the Norn. 'Down, no. The shell is still intact. I've had the architects out there, and they say it could easily be made habitable again. Of course, the best builders in the world were the Giants, and they're all dead now, but they were always expensive and difficult to work with . . .'

That, Malcolm felt, was something of an understatement. Nevertheless, the idea seemed curiously attractive, and he went out with the Younger Norn to look at the place.

'You could have tennis-courts here, and maybe a swimming-pool,' said the Norn, pointing with her umbrella to what had once been the Crack of Doom. 'Or if you don't like the idea of that, how about a rock garden? Or an ornamental lake? With real gnomes,' she said dreamily.

'I think I'd rather just have a lawn,' Malcolm replied. 'And some rosebeds.'

The Norn shrugged, and they moved on to inspect the Steps of Unknowing. 'How about a maze?' suggested the Norn. 'Appropriate, really.'

'No,' said Malcolm. 'I think a garage might be rather more use.'

'Please yourself. Anyway, you like the place?'

'Well, it's quiet, and the neighbours aren't too bad. I lived most of my life in Derby,' Malcolm said. 'It's certainly different from there. But it's rather a long way from the shops.'

'I wouldn't have thought that would have worried you, having the Tarnhelm and so on.'

'True,' said Malcolm, 'but sometimes I like to walk or drive, just for a change.'

'No problem,' said the Norn, 'we'll build you a replica of your favourite city. Valhalla New Town, we could call it.'

The thought of a heavenly version of Milton Keynes was almost enough to put Malcolm off the whole idea, but he asked the Norn to get some plans drawn up and hire an architect. The work would be done by the Nibelungs, who would do a perfectly good job without making unreasonable demands, as the Giants had done.

On the way back, they passed the charred stump of a tree, which had once been the World Ash. To their amazement, they saw a couple of green shoots emerging from the dead and blackened wood.

'That tree's been dead ever since Wotan first came on the scene,' said the Norn. 'It represents the Life Force, apparently.'

'Get someone to put one of those little wire cages round it,' said Malcolm. 'We don't want the squirrels getting at it.'

Malcolm returned from his trip to Valhalla feeling rather tired, not by the journey but by the company of the Younger Norn. He sat down in the drawing-room and took his shoes off; he wanted a quick glass of schnapps and ten minutes with the paper before going to bed. He was getting middle-aged, he realised; but such considerations did not really worry him. Youth, he had decided, was not such a big deal after all.

He looked out over the trout-stream and suddenly found himself in tears. For a moment he could not understand why; but then he realised what had caused what was, generally speaking, an unusual display of emotion. The trout-stream had reminded him of Flosshilde, whom he missed even more than the shoe-inspecting Valkyrie. He had treated Flosshilde very badly . . . No, it wasn't guilt that was making him cry. He had shut it out of his mind for so long that he imagined that it had gone away, but now he knew what his real problem was.

He had heard a story about a man who had gone through life thinking that the word Lunch meant the sun, and it occurred to him that he had been in roughly the same situation himself. Until very recently, he had not known what the word Love really meant; he had thought it referred to the self-deceptive and futile emotion that had plagued him since he first had enough hair on his chin to justify buying a razor of his own. On the night of the confrontation with Wotan, he had suddenly realised his mistake; he had loved Flosshilde then, just at the very moment when she had ceased to exist. So horrible had that thought been that he had excluded it from his brain; but now it had come back and taken him by surprise, and he could see no way of ever getting rid of it. The sorrow he had felt for Ortlinde was little more than sympathy, but he needed the Rhinedaughter. The thought of going to live in Valhalla or being the ruler of the Universe without having her there was unbearable; the thought of being alive without having her there was bad enough.

He shook his head and poured out some more schnapps. Many momentous and terrible things had happened and the Gods had all gone down, just to teach Malcolm Fisher the meaning of the word Love. Had he paid more attention to his English teacher at school, he reflected, the whole world might have been saved a great deal of trouble. He picked up the local paper, and saw a photograph of a tall girl and a man with large ears standing outside a church. Liz Ayres had married Philip Wilcox. He smiled, for this fact meant nothing to him at all. The sooner he got out of this house, the better.

Someone had left the french windows open. He got up and closed them, for the night was cold; summer had passed, and it would be unethical of him to extend it for his own convenience. It had been a strange season, he reflected, and it was just as well that it was over now. The world could cool down again, and he could allow it to rain with a clear conscience.

'Why am I doing all this?' he said aloud.

Now at last he understood. It was blindingly obvious, but because he was so stupid he hadn't seen it before. The world, now God-free and generally purified, was no longer his to hold on to. He must give the Ring to his sister Bridget. She, after all, was older than him, and much cleverer, and generally better equipped to handle difficult problems. He was only the intermediary. Everything fell into place, and he felt as if a great burden had fallen from his shoulders. If only he had done it before, Flosshilde would not have gone down and he might even have had a happy ending of his own; but he had been foolish and wilful, just as his mother would have expected. He had suffered his punishment, and now there was no time to lose. As he had said himself, Bridget was the member of the Fisher family who most resembled the glorious Siegfried. It explained why Ingolf had been so surprised when he had heard his name; he had been expecting *Bridget* Fisher on that fateful night.

He looked at his watch, trying to calculate what time it would be in Sydney. Hadn't Mother Earth herself said something about the Ring rightfully being Bridget's property, because she was the eldest? It would, of course, be difficult to explain it all, for his word carried little credibility with his immediate family; if he said something, they naturally assumed the reverse to be true. But Bridget was wise and would immediately understand, even if his mother didn't. With luck, they would let him keep the Tarnhelm, but if Bridget needed it of course she must have it. He swallowed the rest of his drink and called for an overcoat.

He looked quickly in the mirror to make sure that his hair was neat and tidy (his mother was most particular about such things) and saw to his astonishment that he didn't look like Malcolm Fisher at all. Then he remembered that he was still wearing the Tarnhelm. He would need that to get to Australia, but he might as well stop pretending to be somebody he wasn't.

'Right,' he commanded, 'back to normal.'

The image in the mirror didn't change. It was still the Siegfried face he had been wearing for so long.

'Back to Malcolm Fisher,' he said irritably. 'Come on, jump to it.'

No change. Angrily, he felt for the little buckle under his chin, which he hadn't even noticed for so long now. It came away easily, and he pulled the chainmail cap off and tossed it onto the sofa.

No change. The face that stared stupidly at him out of the mirror was the face of Fafner's Bane, Siegfried the Volsung. He groaned, and knelt down on the floor. Once again, his mother had been proved right. He had stuck like it. From now until the day he died, he was going to have to go around with the evidence of his deceit literally written all over his face.

Worse, he could not even remember what he really looked like. If he knew that, he might be able to get some sort of clever mask made. But the picture had completely vanished from his mind. He picked up the Tarnhelm and gazed at it hopelessly, feeling as he had done when, as a child, he had broken a window or scratched the paint. He had done something awful which he could not put right, and it was all his fault.

The next morning was bright and cold, and Malcolm woke early with a headache, which he prosaically blamed on the schnapps. To clear his head, he strolled down by the trout-stream and stood for a while kicking stones into the water.

'Do you mind?' said a girl's voice.

He knew that voice. He tried hard not to recognise it, because the girl it had belonged to had gone up in a cloud of

211

theology, along with the rest of the High Gods. He had sent his two ravens out looking for the owner of that voice, and they had searched the earth for many days without finding her. She no longer existed, except in the memories of a few unusual people. So what was she doing in his trout-stream?

'Is that you?' he said stupidly.

'Of course it's me,' said the voice irritably. 'Who do you think it was, the *Bismarck*?'

He scrambled down the bank, slipped, and fell in the water. As he did so, it occurred to him that he couldn't swim, and he had forgotten that the trout-stream was only two feet deep. In his panic, he also forgot about the Tarnhelm, and had already resigned himself to the prospect of death by drowning when Flosshilde fished him out.

'Sorry,' she said. 'Did I startle you?'

That was one hell of a leading question, and rather than try and phrase an answer that might not be held against him in future, he replied by throwing his arms around her and kissing her, clumsily but effectively. It had not entered his mind that she might object to this; luckily, she seemed to like it.

'Where the hell have you been?' he said at last.

Flosshilde grinned. 'Did you miss me?' she asked superfluously.

'I thought you'd been zapped,' he said.

'Oh. So you have missed me.'

'Of course I've bloody missed you. Where have you been?'

'On holiday.'

'On *holiday*.'

'Yes,' said Flosshilde, and she could not understand why Malcolm found this so strange. 'We'd planned to go to the Nile Delta again this year, but then that Ortlinde business blew up and by the time it was all over everywhere was full. So we went and stayed with our cousins on the seabed. It was rather boring actually. They're terribly stuffy people, and they've got a pipeline running right through

212

the middle of their sitting-room.'

'So that's why Thought and Memory couldn't find you.'

'Were they looking?'

'They've been doing little else since you vanished. You might have let me know.'

Flosshilde grinned again. 'I didn't know you cared. Honestly, I didn't. I only came back to look for a comb I'd left behind.'

That was not strictly true, except for the bit about the comb, but she hoped he wouldn't notice. It had been no fun at all on the seabed and she hadn't been able to get him out of her mind. His reaction to her last remark was therefore likely to be rather important.

'Well, I do care. I care a whole lot.'

'Yes,' said Flosshilde, remembering the scramble down the bank and the kiss, 'I think you probably do. Snap. By the way, you're all wet.'

'Am I?'

'Yes. Perhaps it would be a good idea if we got out of the water.'

Malcolm could see no reason for this, for he was happier standing in two feet of water with the girl he loved and needed than he had ever been on dry land. But if she thought it would be a good idea, he was willing to give it a try. They climbed out and sat down under a tree. It so happened that it was the same tree that Ortlinde had been standing under when he had first kissed her, but he couldn't be expected to remember everything.

'Let's not talk about it,' Flosshilde said. 'You know what that leads to. Let's just have a nice time for the rest of our lives.'

Put like that, it seemed perfectly simple. Malcolm leaned back against the oak tree and thought about it for a moment. Whatever he felt like doing was probably right. He had that on the very best authority.

'Fair enough,' he said. 'But first I must give the Ring to my sister Bridget.'

'Don't be silly.'

'But I've got to. You see . . .'

'Don't be *silly*.'

'All right, then,' Malcolm said. 'I'll give it to you.'

He took off the Ring, looked at it for a moment, tossed it up in the air, caught it again, and slipped it onto the fourth finger of her left hand. Then he waited for a second. Nothing happened. Flosshilde stared at him with her mouth wide open.

'It suits you,' he said.

'What did you do that for?'

'First,' said Malcolm, 'because it was originally yours. Second, because you're much older and cleverer than I am. Third, because I love you. Fourth, because it's worth it just to see the look on your face.'

Flosshilde could think of nothing to say, and Malcolm savoured the moment. It was probably the last moment of silence he could expect from her for many, many years.

'Are you sure?' said Flosshilde.

Malcolm started to laugh, for it had been Ortlinde's favourite phrase, and soon Flosshilde was giggling too. 'No, but honestly,' she said, 'it's the Ring. Be serious for a moment.'

'Serious?' Malcolm grabbed her arm and pulled her close. 'Don't you see? That's the last thing in the world I can afford to be. Ever since you went away, something terrible has been happening to me. I couldn't think what it was, even though everyone was trying to tell me. Even the Tarnhelm. I was turning into Wotan. I was starting to become just like him.'

'Never,' said Flosshilde. 'You couldn't be. For a start, he was taller than you.'

'I could, and I nearly did. When I realised it, my first reaction was to give the Ring to my sister Bridget, because everyone always said she was so much more responsible than me. But you were right, that would have been the worst possible thing I could have done. Then you came back, and I suddenly understood. The only person in the world that that thing is safe with is you.'

'Me? But that's impossible. I'm not a nice person at all.'

'Not you as well.'

'No, I mean it. I'm probably not cruel or malicious, but I'm thoughtless and frivolous. I wouldn't take the job seriously, and the world would get into an awful mess. I'd forget to make it rain at the right time, because I'd always want it to be fine for sunbathing, and if I was bored with it being January, I'd make it July again, and then everything would get out of gear. I'd be hopeless at it, really.'

'That's what I thought when I started. And it hasn't turned out too badly, has it?'

Flosshilde frowned and bit her lip, a manoeuvre she had often practised in front of the mirror. 'Oh, go on, then,' she said, 'just to please you I will.'

'That,' said Malcolm triumphantly, 'is the best possible reason. You've passed. Congratulations.'

'I still think,' said Flosshilde, holding up the Ring to the light to admire it, 'that you're being a bit hasty . . .' She tailed off. 'You're right,' she said. 'It does suit me. It'll go very nicely with that gold evening dress I got in Strasbourg.'

She took one more look at the Ring and promptly dismissed it from her mind, for she had more important things to think about. 'Why the sudden change of heart?' she asked. 'I mean, when I left for the seabed, you were still madly in love with that stuffy old Valkyrie with the interesting shoes. You aren't going to change your mind about me, are you?'

'I hope not,' said Malcolm. 'We'll have to see, won't we?'

'Did I ever tell you the story . . . ?'

'Later.'

'It's a very funny story.'

'Did I ever tell *you* the story of the idiot who ran over a badger?'

'I know that one.'

'But I tell it very well, and it's the only really funny story I know.'

'Go on, then.'

He told her the story and she laughed, although she knew that she could have told it rather better herself. In fact, she could have done his voice rather better than he could. But it didn't matter. This was happiness, she realised, even more than sunbathing or the parties they used to have at Camelot. She was slightly disappointed with herself for being made happy so easily, for she had always thought of herself as a rather glamorous, sophisticated person. Nevertheless, it would do very nicely to be going on with.

Malcolm listened to her laughter, and for the first time in his life he knew that everything was going to be all right. Niceness, he realised, was not enough, and Love was only part of the rest. You had to have laughter, too. Laughter would make everything come out right in the end, or if it didn't nobody would notice. He started to tell her about his plans for the new Valhalla. She liked the idea, and started making suggestions about how the place should be redecorated. These mostly seemed to consist of swimming-pools, flumes and ornamental lakes, and he realised that sooner or later he was going to have to learn how to swim. The thought made him shudder, but he put it on one side.

'By the way,' he said. 'I suppose you're immortal.'

'I think so. Why?'

'Isn't that going to make it rather difficult for me? You see, I'm not.'

Flosshilde shook her head. 'I solved that one some time ago,' she said.

'Did you now? That was thoughtful of you.'

Flosshilde blushed, spontaneously for once, and realised that she hadn't quite timed it right, which was unusual for her, since she was unquestionably one of the three best blushers in the world. But Malcolm didn't seem to have noticed, and it was nice to be with somebody who didn't

216

criticise when you got things wrong.

'I looked it up in all the books,' she went on, 'and there's no problem. Every time you feel yourself getting old, you just turn yourself into someone younger.'

Malcolm shook his head. 'I don't think the Tarnhelm works any more,' he said sadly, and he told her about his attempts to go back to being Malcolm Fisher. She laughed, and told him not to be so silly.

'Haven't you learnt anything?' she said. 'You tried to turn yourself into Malcolm Fisher. You *are* Malcolm Fisher. Of course it didn't work.'

Malcolm didn't quite follow that, but he was reassured. There didn't seem to be anything else to worry about now, so he suggested that they went in and had some breakfast instead.

'Just a moment,' said Flosshilde.

She looked hard at the Ring, held her breath and pointed at the sky. A small pink cloud appeared out of nowhere, rushing across the sky until it was directly overhead. There was a blinding flash of pink lightning, and the cloud had vanished. The air was filled with pink rose petals, and a flight of flamingos climbed gracefully into the air.

'No,' said Flosshilde, 'maybe not. It seemed like a good idea at the time.'

'It's the thought that counts,' Malcolm said. 'Come on, I'm hungry.'

They walked into the house, and the two ravens who had been eavesdropping from the branches of the oak tree looked at each other.

'I think that's nice,' said Memory.

'Idiot,' said Thought. 'Is that a dead rabbit I can see over there?'

'Where?'

'Just by that patch of nettles.'

'Now you're talking,' said Memory.

They glided down and started to peck. It was a good, meaty rabbit, and they were both hungry. When he had finished, Memory wiped his beak neatly on his leg and stood thoughtfully for a while.

'Did you ever see that film?' he said.

'What film?'

'Can't remember. Anyway, it reminds me a bit of that. Happy ending and all.'

Thought shook his head. 'Don't like happy endings,' he said. 'They're a cop-out. Life's not like that.'

'I dunno,' said Memory. 'Sometimes it is.'

'You're soft, you are,' said Thought scornfully. 'Come on, time we were on our way.'

They sailed up into the sky, and began their day's patrol. Wherever life was stirring and brains were working they flew, their bright round eyes missing nothing, their ears constantly alert. But today was going to be another quiet day in the best of all possible worlds. After a while they grew bored, and turned back. As they flew over the little village of Ralegh's Cross, they saw three workmen with pickaxes trying to break up a strange outcrop of rock which had appeared in the middle of the road some months earlier. But their tools would not bite on the hard stone, and they had given it up for a while.

'What I want to know is,' said one of the men, 'how did it get there in the first place?'

Memory dived down and perched on the rock which had once been the Giant Ingolf. 'It's a long story,' he said.

But the man wasn't listening.